TIMEOUT!

HEADS UP, HOOPS FANS.

HEAD-TO-HEAD BASKETBALL is a very different kind of book; it can be read frontwards or backwards. Start from one end and you'll get the inside stuff on the New York Knicks' all-star center, Patrick Ewing. Or start from the other side to get the lowdown on the Charlotte Hornets' big man, Alonzo Mourning.

Whichever way you begin, you'll want to read *both* superstar stories *before* jumping into the amazing middle section of the book. Read how Patrick and Alonzo battle on the court — but remain great friends off it — *then* check out the fantastic photos, stats, and comic strip that shows just how these two NBA giants stack up against each other.

Ok, it's tip-off time. So pick Alonzo or Patrick and get ready for all the Head-to-Head action!

PATRICK EWING

by Neil Cohen

A *Sports Illustrated For Kids* Book

Bantam Books

NEW YORK • TORONTO • LONDON • SYDNEY • AUCKLAND

Head-to-Head Basketball: Patrick Ewing and Alonzo Mourning
by Neil Cohen

A Bantam Book/November 1994

Sports Illustrated For Kids and **Sports Illustrated KiDS** are registered trademarks of Time Inc. Sports Illustrated For Kids Books are published in cooperation with Bantam Doubleday Dell Publishing Group, Inc. under license from Time Inc.

Cover and interior design by Miriam Dustin

For information address: Bantam Books

ISBN 0-553-48165-7

Published simultaneously in the United States and Canada

Bantam books are published by Bantam Books, a division of Bantam Doubleday Dell Publishing Group, Inc. Its trademark, consisting of the words "Bantam Books" and the portrayal of a rooster, is Registered in the U.S. Patent and Trademark Office and in other countries. Marca Registrada. Bantam Books, 1540 Broadway, New York, NY 10036

Printed in the United States of America

CWO 0 9 8 7 6 5 4 3 2

CONTENTS

FRIENDS
◆ ◆ ◆ AND FOES

Madison Square Garden, the home arena of the New York Knickerbockers, was shaking. The sellout crowd of 19,763 was on its feet, waving souvenir towels and urging the Knicks on. It was May 12, 1993, and the Knicks and the Charlotte Hornets were locked in Game 2 of their best-of-seven Eastern Conference semifinal playoff series.

Patrick Ewing, the Knicks' seven-foot center and cocaptain, looked up at the giant scoreboard hanging in the rafters of the Garden. It showed that the Knicks were trailing the Hornets by 13 points with just 6 minutes 48 seconds to play.

Patrick wiped the sweat from his forehead. Thanks to his scoring, the Knicks had held a seven-point lead midway through the third quarter. Since then, Charlotte had outscored New York by 20 points and were kicking the Knicks' butts on their own home court.

This was a big game for Patrick and the Knicks in their quest for an NBA championship. They had finished the regular season with the best record in the league and had defeated the Indiana Pacers in the first round of the playoffs. The Knicks had won the first game of their series with the Hornets, but it was important that they win the second, too, before going to Charlotte to play the next two games on the Hornets' unfriendly homecourt, the Hive.

But there was even more to it than that. This series was Patrick's first post-season head-to-head confrontation with Alonzo Mourning, the Hornets' 6'10" rookie center. Alonzo was one of a group of outstanding young centers who had recently come into the league and were challenging Patrick's status as one of the top centers in the game.

Although they were eight years apart in age, Patrick and Alonzo were also the best of friends. Alonzo had idolized Patrick when he was in high school and Patrick was a star at Georgetown University. Alonzo had gone to college at Georgetown, and he and Patrick had spent summers practicing with and playing against each other in the Georgetown gym. Now they were both stars in the NBA, playing in one of the biggest games of their professional careers.

Ever since he had joined the National Basketball Association eight years earlier, Patrick had been carrying the Knicks on his shoulders. Now, with the team down by 13 points, he would have to come through in the clutch again.

• He tried to lift their play by playing as hard as he could, and his teammates responded. The Knick defense shut down the Hornet offense. But they still trailed by five points, 93–88, and now there were only 90 seconds left in the game! It was time for Patrick to use his head as well as his strength.

When the Hornets sent two players to guard Patrick, Patrick found the open man and made a nice pass to Hubert Davis, the Knicks' rookie guard. Hubert drove for a layup to make the score 93–90 with 1:20 left to play.

After the Hornets failed to score, Patrick again beat the double-team and passed the ball to Hubert, who was open behind the three-point shooting line. With just 44.3 seconds left, Hubert launched a 25-footer. The shot was good! The game was tied and going into overtime! The crowd was going crazy!

The two teams traded the lead back and forth in the five-minute overtime period. Then Patrick took charge again. With just 35.7 seconds to play, Patrick took a pass from Hubert and launched one of his trademark 15-foot jump shots. The ball sailed through the basket! The Knicks led, 101–99.

Alonzo had a chance to tie the game for the Hornets, but he missed a three-point shot. When the Knicks got the rebound, Patrick sprinted downcourt on a fast break and scored on a big slam dunk as the crowd went wild. The game was over! The Knicks had won 105–101. Patrick led the winners with 34 points and 11 rebounds.

"It was an incredible, incredible, incredible win," said Knick coach Pat Riley after the game. "I've been in 150 to 200 playoff games, but I've never seen anything quite like this."

The Knicks would go on to win the series from Charlotte, four games to one. After the final game, Patrick and Alonzo met at halfcourt and gave each other a big hug. The Knicks would advance to the next round of the playoffs. The Hornets would go home and wait for next season.

"It's rewarding to live up to our expectations," Patrick told reporters in the lockerroom after the final game. "This series was like the whole year for us. It was a war. I'm glad it's over."

When a reporter asked what he had said to Patrick after the game, Alonzo responded, "I wished him luck. I'm definitely rooting for the Knicks because of Patrick. He deserves it. He definitely deserves a title."

The title would not come to Patrick that season, however. In the Eastern Conference finals, the Knicks battled bravely but fell to the Chicago Bulls in six games.

Patrick, who had won three state championships in high school and a national championship in college, would have to work harder to get what he now wanted more than anything: his first NBA title.

But Patrick still had faith in the words of advice his parents once told him: "Whatever you do, if you put the time in to work at it, you will succeed."

Living by those words had already carried Patrick a long way from where his life had begun.

COMING TO AMERICA

Patrick Aloysius Ewing was born in Kingston, Jamaica, on August 5, 1962. Jamaica is an island in the Caribbean Sea, located about 480 miles south of Florida. Kingston is the capital city of Jamaica. Jamaica has a tropical climate, which means it feels like summer there all year long. It has mountains and beautiful beaches. People from around the world come to Jamaica in the winter to take vacations.

But, despite the weather, many Jamaicans have a hard life. Some live in shacks and have to scrape out a living from farming, mining, or serving tourists. Few parents can afford to send their children to college.

Patrick is the fifth of seven children born to Carl and Dorothy Ewing. Patrick has an older brother, three older sisters, and two younger sisters. Mr. Ewing worked as a car mechanic. The Ewings lived in a house that had no telephone and no indoor bathroom.

Patrick remembers playing with his friends in the warm sunshine. His favorite sports were soccer and cricket. Cricket is a sport like baseball. Patrick was a fast runner and a good jumper. "I wanted to be a professional soccer player," he says.

Besides playing sports, Patrick also loved to draw pictures. He would copy the comic strip characters out of the Sunday newspaper or have his mother pose for him while he drew her picture.

When Patrick was eight, his parents decided to move the family to the United States. They wanted their children to get a better education than they could get in Jamaica.

But moving a family of nine to another country was difficult. In 1971, Mrs. Ewing left Jamaica for the United States to find a job and a place for the family to live. She chose Cambridge, Massachusetts, because the city has many West Indians, as people from the Caribbean islands are known. Cambridge is right across the Charles River from Boston, the largest city in Massachusetts.

Mrs. Ewing found a job working in the cafeteria of a hospital. Soon, the other members of the family began joining her in Cambridge, two or three at a time. Mr. Ewing found a job in a factory that made rubber hoses. Meanwhile, Patrick stayed with his grandmother in Kingston until it was his turn. "It was hard to be separated [from my parents] like that," he remembers. "But it was something we had to do to make a better life for ourselves."

He arrived in the United States on January 11, 1975, when he was 12 years old. He found the United States to be a strange place. The weather is a lot colder than in Jamaica, something, he says, he still can't get used to. The people spoke English just as he did, but it was a different kind of English, with its own words and its own way of using the words in sentences. The way one language is spoken differently in a particular place is called a dialect.

There was another strange thing about the United States: the games kids played. In Cambridge, the big sport was basketball. Patrick had never seen a basketball before!

On his way home from school, Patrick would stop and watch the neighborhood kids play basketball in a schoolyard. Patrick was already tall, so one day, the kids asked him if he wanted to join the game. Patrick agreed, but he soon found out that playing this new game was not easy. "It was the most difficult thing I've ever done," he says now.

Patrick was clumsy on the court and the other kids made fun of him. They expected a tall kid to be a good basketball player. "There were times I wanted to quit," Patrick remembers. "I got so tired of people teasing me."

Why didn't Patrick give up basketball? "I loved it so much," he says. "So I said, forget them, it doesn't matter what they say, just so long as I liked playing."

For many hours, nearly every day, Patrick was at

the schoolyard, playing in games or practicing his shooting and dribbling. Little by little, he began to improve.

He also began to grow. Patrick was 6'1" when he
was 13. But over the next summer, Patrick grew five inches to become 6'6". By the time he was an 11th grader at
Cambridge Rindge and Latin High School, a private
Catholic school, Patrick had grown to be 6'11". By 12th
grade, he was 7' tall.

With Patrick playing center, Rindge and Latin won
77 games and lost only 1 during his three years with the
varsity team. The school won three state championships!

In high school, Patrick began to wear a T-shirt
under his basketball jersey. He would do that in college,
too, where he would launch a fashion trend. It started
because Rindge and Latin was playing a game on a court
that was laid on top of an ice rink, and Patrick was cold.
Soon, his teammates began wearing T-shirts under their
jerseys, too.

Patrick's high school coach, Mike Jarvis, taught
Patrick a lot about playing basketball. Coach Jarvis was an
admirer of Bill Russell, the center who led the Boston
Celtics to 11 NBA titles in 13 seasons in the 1950's and
1960's. Bill was not a great scorer. He won games by playing great defense.

Coach Jarvis taught Patrick to play the same way.
Patrick never averaged more than 21 points per game in
high school, although he could have scored many more.

Instead, he passed the ball to his teammates, played tough defense, and ran up and down the court, sometimes blocking a shot on defense to start a fast break, then finishing the play with a slam dunk into his opponents' basket.

In 1979, Patrick became a United States citizen. (To become a citizen, you must get permission from the government to live in the U.S. Then you must wait five years and pass a citizenship test of ten questions about the United States.) He was invited to try out for the 1980 Olympic basketball team — even though he was only a high school junior. Back then, the Olympic team was made up of the best college players in the country. (Patrick didn't make the team.)

Patrick worked as hard in the classroom as he did on the court. He had some difficulties in school, particularly in reading. From junior high school on, he needed tutors to help him.

But Patrick kept up with his class. "In all his time at high school, Patrick never missed a class or a study hall, or one practice," said Coach Jarvis. "He was a great student because he would ask questions. And if he didn't understand the answer, he would ask again."

Patrick was considered the best high school basketball player in the country and many colleges wanted to offer him an athletic scholarship. His family wanted Patrick to choose the college that would give him the best education. Between Patrick's junior and senior years, Coach Jarvis sent letters to 150 schools, telling them that if Patrick were to come to their school, he would need special attention in the classroom: tutors, tapes of lessons, and extra time to take exams.

Unfortunately, that letter was printed in the newspapers. Patrick had always been booed when Rindge and Latin played games at other schools because he was so much better than anyone else. But now, those students from other schools started teasing Patrick, too. They called him names and made fun of his learning problems. Patrick became angry and got into fights with rival players. Then he decided instead to make those students' pay for their cruelty by beating their teams even worse on the court.

Even as they booed him and teased him, many kids around the Boston area were hoping that Patrick would choose to attend Boston College or Boston University. They wanted him to stay in Boston and turn one of the local schools into a winner. But another college in another city had won over Patrick and his parents: Georgetown University in Washington, D.C. They were impressed by Georgetown coach John Thompson.

Coach Thompson is an African-American who not only is a good basketball coach, but who also makes sure his players graduate. He is also a big man, like his players, at 6'10". Patrick and his family thought Patrick could learn a lot from Coach Thompson: about basketball and life.

In June 1980, Patrick graduated from high school. That summer he moved away from home for the first time, to attend Georgetown. Just five and a half years after arriving in the United States from Jamaica, he was embarking on the next big journey of his life.

HEAD TO HEAD

When Patrick graduated high school in Cambridge, Massachusetts, at age 17, Alonzo Mourning was a 10-year-old fourth-grader in Chesapeake, Virginia. Patrick was the best high school player in the country. Alonzo didn't care much for basketball; his sport was football.

THE HOYA
DESTROYA

Imagine how you'd feel if the whole country was watching to see if you would become the best basketball player ever. You'd feel excited but lonely, and a little afraid.

That's probably how 18-year-old Patrick Ewing felt as he left home in the summer of 1981 to begin classes at Georgetown University. Georgetown is located in Washington, D.C., the capital of the United States. Washington, D.C. is on the border of the states of Maryland and Virginia. It is the home of the President, the Senate and the House of Representatives, the Supreme Court, and many other government offices.

But Patrick seemed to be the most famous person in town. Sports reporters wanted to interview him all the time. Georgetown coach John Thompson tried to protect Patrick from the media. He made it hard for reporters to find Patrick. Even when the reporters could find him, Patrick often did not want to answer questions.

Patrick was a shy young man who just wanted to go

to class and play basketball. He was always polite, but he didn't like telling reporters anything personal about his life. Some sportswriters weren't used to that. The stories they wrote sometimes gave the impression that Patrick wouldn't talk because he didn't like people, or wasn't smart enough to have anything to say.

Patrick was also misunderstood by fans of opposing teams. Georgetown played in the Big East Conference, and some fans at Big East schools remembered the letter that Patrick's high school coach had sent to colleges. They would hold up signs saying things like "Ewing Can't Read This."

The people who got to know Patrick liked him. His teammates found him to be easy-going, funny, and smart. Opponents would come to play Georgetown, thinking that Patrick was some kind of shot-blocking robot. Once they got to know him, they found him to be a very likable guy. Many players imitated the way Patrick dressed during games, wearing T-shirts under their uniform jerseys.

On the basketball court, Patrick was all business. The Georgetown sports teams are nicknamed the Hoyas. Hoya is a Latin word that means "What rocks!" Patrick soon became known as the "Hoya Destroya," for the way his shot blocking destroyed opponents' hopes of scoring. He was also known as the "Beast of the East."

The Hoyas took a lot of pride in stopping other teams from scoring. Coach Thompson had been a teammate of Bill Russell's on the Boston Celtics, and like Patrick's high school coach, he talked to Patrick about how the great Celtic center played defense. Bill did not just block shots and knock them out of bounds. He would tip the ball over to a teammate to start a fast break and get an easy basket.

Patrick tried to play that way, too. But despite what he had heard from his coaches, he didn't want to be the next Bill Russell. "I want to be Patrick Ewing," he said.

As the Georgetown center, Patrick's job was to guard the basket. It was not to take outside jump shots. But after practice, he would stay at the gym, working on his jump shots, dribbling, and other moves he would need when he joined the NBA.

Patrick did not score a lot of points for a great player. During his four seasons as a Hoya, he averaged just 15.3 points per game. But with his all-around play, he helped the Hoyas win 121 games, while losing only 23.

In his freshman season, Patrick teamed up with future NBA guard Eric "Sleepy" Floyd to lead Georgetown all the way to the 1982 NCAA tournament championship game. In that game, the Hoyas faced the North Carolina Tar Heels, which had three future NBA stars: Sam Perkins, James Worthy, and a freshman named Michael Jordan.

Patrick was a little too up for the game when it began. He blocked North Carolina's first four shots, but was called for goaltending each time. Later, in one of the most exciting finishes ever, North Carolina won the national championship when Michael hit a jump shot with just seconds left to play.

It was a crushing defeat for the Hoyas but it made Patrick determined to return to the championship game and win!

In the classroom, Patrick followed his love for drawing and became a fine arts major. Fine arts is the study of painting and sculpture. Patrick enjoyed painting landscapes, which are pictures of what places look like: a seashore, mountains, even a city.

During summers, he worked as a student assistant in a government office on Capitol Hill, where the Senate and House of Representatives are. There, he met a young woman named Rita Williams, who became his girlfriend.

After every basketball season, reporters would ask Patrick if he was going to leave school early to join the NBA. Patrick knew he could earn millions of dollars, but he also knew how much his parents wanted him to get a college education. "Money's never been the most important thing in my life," he once said. Patrick became even more determined to graduate as he began his junior year. At the start of the school term, his mother died.

In a season of inspired play, Patrick led Georgetown to its first national championship. The Hoyas defeated the University of Houston in the 1984 NCAA championship game. The Houston Cougars were led by Hakeem (then Akeem) Olajuwon and Clyde Drexler.

That summer, Patrick was invited to play on the United States Olympic basketball team that would be competing in the 1984 Summer Olympics in Los Angeles, California. Patrick teamed with Michael Jordan to help the U.S. win the gold medal.

When Patrick began his senior year, Georgetown was rated as the best team in the country and expected to win a second straight national title. No team had won two straight championships since UCLA had done it in 1972–1973. (Duke University would do it in 1991–1992.)

Patrick was considered to be the best college basketball player in the country. But he had grown to be more than that. He was no longer a shy 18-year-old but a mature 22-year-old. He was the team's leader on the court. Off the court, he was bright and well-spoken if still not always willing to answer reporters' questions. That, he felt, was his right. He is "more proud of being a man than this great basketball player we talk about," said Coach Thompson.

Patrick led the Hoyas to another great year, and their third appearance in the NCAA tournament's Final Four in his four seasons. But in the 1985 championship game, Georgetown was upset by the Villanova University Wildcats. It was a disappointing ending to a great college career, but Patrick handled it like a man. He stood and applauded when the Wildcats received their championship trophy after the game.

Patrick was named college player of the year and a first-team All-America for the third time in his college career. For his four years at Georgetown, Patrick finished his career as the school's leading career rebounder (1,316), shot-blocker (493) and second-leading scorer (2,184).

Pro basketball scouts said Patrick was sure to be the first pick in the 1985 NBA draft. They believed he could turn a bad team into a good one all by himself.

NBA teams wanted Patrick so badly that the league started a lottery to determine who would get the first pick. In the past, the team with the worst record picked first, but the league was worried that teams would lose games on purpose to get Patrick. With a lottery, the seven worst teams all had a chance to get the first pick.

In May 1985, Patrick graduated from Georgetown with a degree in fine arts. His father, brother, sisters, and Coach Thompson were there to watch him receive his degree. He was proud and he knew his mother would have been proud, too.

"I've learned a great deal at Georgetown," he said. "Maturity, that's what college is for. Another thing my mother said was to put something away for a rainy day. I have to be able to work, to do something with my life. I won't stop existing once I stop playing basketball. "

That month, the New York Knicks won the NBA lottery. At the June 18 draft they selected Patrick with the first pick, and later that summer signed him to a 10-year contract worth about $30 million dollars.

Patrick had certainly shown those people who said he was too dumb to read and too awkward to play basketball. Through hard work, he had made himself into a college graduate and a millionaire!

HEAD TO HEAD

Both Patrick and Alonzo graduated from Georgetown University, which plays basketball in the Big East Conference. Schools that play basketball in the Big East are Boston College, the University of Connecticut, the University of Miami, the University of Pittsburgh, Providence College, Seton Hall University, St. John's University, Syracuse University, and Villanova University. Rutgers University, the University of Virginia, and Notre Dame will join the Big East for basketball for the 1995–96 season.

NEW YORK
BLUES

Few players have ever joined a professional sports team with more pressure on them than Patrick Ewing had in his rookie season with the New York Knicks, in the fall of 1985.

Patrick was just 23 years old and had never played a game in the NBA. But many people expected him to lead the Knicks to a championship right away! One of the New York newspapers called him "St. Patrick," and Madison Square Garden "St. Patrick's Cathedral."

New York is not only one of the largest cities in the world, with a population of more than seven million people, it is also the media capital of the world. Patrick Ewing coming to the Knicks was big news. Newspapers, magazines, radio stations, and TV stations were watching everything he did.

Soon after he signed with the Knicks, one of the newspapers found out that Patrick had fathered a son while he was in college at Georgetown. The boy's name was Patrick Junior, and he lived in Cambridge with his mother, who had been Patrick's girlfriend in high school. Patrick and the boy's mother did not plan to marry, but Patrick was helping to raise his son.

Patrick said he had tried to keep the fact that he had a son, who was now 1 year old, a secret because he wanted his son to have a normal life. But soon newspaper headlines revealed his secret to everyone in the country. In spite of all the stories and questions, Patrick remained quiet about his child. "He's my son and I love him, and that's all I'd like to say about that."

Patrick worked hard to prepare for his New York debut. He spent the summer at Georgetown, practicing almost every day against current and former Hoya players — the bigger the better. He played against big and strong players because that was what he expected to find in the NBA. But nothing could have prepared Patrick for what he would find once he joined the Knicks.

Nobody in the NBA, no matter how good a player he is, can win a championship all by himself. NBA teams are just too good for any one player to come in and dominate the league for an entire season. Not even Superman could come in and make the 1985–86 Knicks into a winner.

The Knicks were coming off a 24–58 season, their worst in 21 years. And their two best returning players, forward Bernard King and center Bill Cartwright, would be out for the season with injuries.

Besides, Patrick himself had a lot to learn about playing at the highest level of the game. The players were bigger than any he had faced before, so he could not just jump over everyone to get rebounds. They also were quicker, so they could double-team him and force him to make turnovers. And they were simply better basketball players, so he could not try to block every shot; they would fool him with a head fake and then drive around him for an easy basket.

In Patrick's first regular season game, (which was shown on national television) he was taught some lessons by Moses Malone, the veteran center of the Philadelphia 76ers. Moses, although two inches shorter than Patrick, outscored the rookie, 35–18, and out-rebounded him, 13–6, as the Sixers went on to win the game.

Still, Patrick had the potential to be a great pro player. He showed that he was a much better shooter than he was in college, unveiling a deadly turnaround jump shot. He soon became the Knicks' leading scorer and rebounder, averaging more than 20 points and 9 rebounds per game.

However, he didn't get much help from his teammates, and the Knicks lost their first eight games of the season. Before mid-season, the Knicks had already lost more games than all of Patrick's teams had lost in his entire life, high school and college put together! Patrick didn't complain. But he did say, "I don't like losing and I don't want to get used to it."

Away from the court, Patrick tried to find peace. He moved into an apartment across the Hudson River in New Jersey. On weekends, his girlfriend, Rita, who was now a law student at Georgetown, sometimes would visit. Most of the time, Patrick listened to music, and cooked Jamaican dishes, like curried goat and rice and peas.

He tried to have some fun and enjoy being a celebrity. He appeared as a guest on a television show called *Webster* and as a guest vee-jay on MTV. He also helped Adidas, the sneaker company he endorsed, with its "Stay in School" program for kids.

Patrick always signed autographs for kids. And reporters and players around the NBA found him to be a much nicer guy than they had expected. His teammates called him a "regular guy." Knick coach Hubie Brown said even if he wasn't so talented, every coach would want him "because he's a pleasure to be around."

On the court, Patrick tried to carry the team all by himself, but his body began to break down under the strain. The Knicks won three games in a row late in November, but then Patrick sprained an ankle and was out of the lineup. They put together another winning streak when he returned, but in the final minutes of a double-overtime win over the Boston Celtics on Christmas Day, Patrick sprained his right knee, and and had to sit out again.

Patrick was chosen for the 1986 NBA All-Star Game in February, but he reinjured his right knee and had to miss the game. He tried playing even though the knee hurt, only to injure it again in March. This time, the Knick team doctor decided that Patrick needed knee surgery, and would have to miss the final two months of the season.

Despite this setback, Patrick led all rookies in scoring and rebounding, and was named NBA Rookie of the Year after the 1985-86 season. But he was not satisfied because the Knicks had done poorly and finished with a record of 23–59.

During the summer, Patrick was back at the Georgetown gym, lifting weights to make himself stronger.

Patrick hoped 1986–87 would be a better season for the Knicks. For one thing, Bill Cartwright would be back. But that turned out to be more of a problem than a solution.

Coach Brown wanted to play Patrick and Bill at the same time. Both men are 7-feet tall, and Coach Brown believed that together they would get a lot of rebounds, block a lot of shots, and make it hard for other teams to defend against them.

The coach wanted Bill to play center and Patrick to play power forward, a position that had Patrick moving around the court a lot more. But Patrick did not seem suited to play forward. Because he had to play away from the basket, his scoring and rebounding dropped off. On defense, he was getting beaten by smaller, quicker players who could drive right by him. The result was that the Knicks kept losing.

In addition, both of Patrick's knees had started to bother him. He had to rest his knees at practice so he would be able to play in games. This annoyed Coach Brown, who thought that Patrick was sitting because he didn't want to play forward.

Coach Brown was under a lot of pressure because the team was still losing even after it had spent so much money on Patrick. He criticized Patrick in the newspapers.

Patrick didn't like to see his coach blasting him in the press. He felt that if Coach Brown had a problem, the two of them should talk about it. Patrick said he didn't like playing forward, but that he always gave his all no matter what. "I play hard every night," Patrick said, "and, when that's not true any longer, I'll retire. That has been the case from the first game I played."

In December, with the Knicks floundering with a 4–12 record, Hubie Brown was fired as Knick head coach and replaced by assistant coach Bob Hill.

Right away, Coach Hill moved Patrick back to center and used Bill coming off the bench. Patrick responded by having a great December, averaging 22 points and almost 10 rebounds over 13 games. He was named NBA Player of the Week for the last week in December, when he led the Knicks on a three-game winning streak.

Patrick had started to wear contact lenses, which seemed to help his shooting. He increased his scoring, which had been 13.1 points per game under Hubie Brown, to 21.5.

The Knicks improved their record to 21-45. But they still were not going to make the playoffs for the third year in a row, and fans began to take out their impatience on Patrick.

For a game on St. Patrick's Day, the Knicks gave out life-sized posters of Patrick. Patrick, unfortunately, had a bad game. Many fans rolled up their posters and threw them down onto the court in disgust. Coach Hill remembers that Patrick tried to appear as if the fans' actions didn't bother him, but that he was sure it was hard for the young center to be treated that way.

Then in an overtime win against the Indiana Pacers later in March, Patrick slipped on a wet spot on the court floor, and sprained a ligament in his left knee. (A ligament is a band of body tissue that holds bones and organs in place.) Patrick was once again out for the season.

When doctors examined Patrick, they discovered why he was having so many problems with his knees. He has a painful condition called chondromalacia, which is a wearing out of the cartilage (another kind of body tissue) that surrounds the knee. Patrick has learned to ice his knees after games, and just to play with the pain.

Talk about bad luck. In Patrick's first two seasons in New York, things had gone from bad to worse.

HEAD TO HEAD

While Patrick struggled in his first two seasons with the Knicks, Alonzo was emerging as the best high school player in the country. In his junior season, 1986–87, he led his school to the state championship.

GLIMPSE OF GLORY

In the spring of 1987, the Knicks hired a new general manager and a new coach. The new general manager (the person who makes the trades and salary decisions for the team), Al Bianchi, promised to bring to New York players who would help Patrick win a championship. The new coach, Rick Pitino, was a man Patrick knew and respected. Suddenly, there was hope.

Coach Pitino had been head basketball coach at Boston University (B.U.) when Patrick was a ninth-grader in Cambridge. Patrick would sometimes visit the B.U. gym to watch the team practice. Coach Pitino was an enthusiastic coach who enjoyed teaching young players the game.

Patrick spent the summer of 1987 in Georgetown, to improve the weaknesses in his game. He worked on another move on offense to go with his jump shot, and developed a hook shot. As a favor to Coach Thompson, he also visited a basketball camp in Princeton, New Jersey to see a high school player named Alonzo Mourning. Alonzo was a big fan of Patrick's. The two became friends and met again when Alonzo's Amateur Athletic Union team practiced at Georgetown later that summer.

He also helped out at the Special Olympics by putting on a basketball clinic for the kids.

When the season began in the fall of 1987, Coach Pitino taught the Knicks a new style of play. He wanted them to play a fast-paced game with lots of fast-breaks and three-point shooting, and a hard-nosed defense that featured a full-court press.

But it would take the Knicks time to learn to play this way. They lost their first five games of the season. Still, opponents noticed that this was a different kind of Knick team. They worked much harder on the court and played with a lot of team spirit.

People who work hard often make their own luck, and that's what happened to the Knicks. In their sixth game, they were down by one point to the Milwaukee Bucks with just 21 seconds to play. Patrick took a jump shot from the baseline. The ball rolled around the rim four times and fell in! The Knicks had won their first game of the season!

Little by little, the Knicks improved. Patrick was helped by the play of rookie point guard Mark Jackson, a good passer who was able to get the ball to Patrick when he was in a position to score. Patrick was selected to play in the NBA All-Star game for the second time in his three pro seasons.

Patrick enjoyed Coach Pitino's style of play. "I'm a better runner than most centers, so it's easier for me to play when I can beat someone up the floor, rather than pushing and shoving with someone 7'1" or 7'4" and 240 pounds," he explained.

By the second half of the season, the Knicks had turned into a good team. They won 24 of their last 40 games, and 20 of 25 games at home in Madison Square Garden.

With his new hook shot, Patrick was becoming an even better scorer. Over one six-game stretch, he scored 36 points or more in four games. For the 1987–88 season, he averaged 20.2 points per game.

When the Knicks beat the Pacers in the last game of the regular season, they piled on top of each other on the court as if they had just won the NBA title. For the first time since Patrick had arrived in New York, the Knicks were going to the playoffs!

Their visit to the playoffs was a short one — the Knicks were beaten by the Celtics in the first round. But they had taken a giant step forward. After the series, Patrick went around the locker room and thanked all the new players for helping the team get this far.

Things were looking up for the Knicks. In June, they traded backup center Bill Cartwright to the Chicago Bulls for power forward Charles Oakley. Charles, who was 6'9", had been the league's top rebounder since he came into the NBA two seasons ago. He would help Patrick under the boards. When the 1988–89 season began, Patrick and Mark Jackson were named co-captains of the team.

The Knicks, however, got off to a slow start, losing their first three games. Patrick's knees were slowing him down and he was getting into foul trouble. When he had to sit, the team lost.

But the Knicks were hustling and playing tough defense, and soon this paid off and they started to win. With Charles Oakley, they now had a strong inside game to go with their pressing, running game. They ran their record to 8–4. By mid-December, the Knicks were in first place in the NBA's Atlantic Division, ahead of the Celtics! The Garden was rocking. Midway through the season, the Knicks were 30–16, the fourth best record in the league!

Patrick was happy to be part of a winning team again. He was playing in every game and working in every practice, even when his knees hurt. When he was on the bench, he would wave his towel and cheer the team on.

Reporters noted that Patrick seemed like a changed man off the court. He was more relaxed talking with them. He seemed to be leaving his serious game-face on the court. Patrick said that he had become more mature as he had gotten older, but that he was still the same person. It was the things around him that had changed!

Patrick was averaging 22.6 points and 9.7 rebounds per game. He made the All-Star team for the third time, and was named NBA Player of the Week at the end of February, when he averaged 29.8 points and 4.5 blocks to lead the Knicks to three wins in four games. In their only loss that week, he scored 45 points, a career high!

He had another 40-point game against the Phoenix Suns in March, as the Knicks ran their home-court winning streak to 24 games. That month, Patrick also sat in the stands and watched the Georgetown Hoyas win the Big East tournament with freshman Alonzo Mourning at center. After the game, Patrick met Alonzo in the tunnel to the player's dressing room and gave him a high five.

It was rare that Patrick wasn't being double-teamed. Sometimes he would try to score anyway and other times he would pass the ball back to the open man. When the open players were able to hit their outside shots, the Knicks would win. When opponents didn't have to worry about the other Knicks, they would drop back and surround Patrick. The other players would still try to pass the ball to Patrick, but their passes were often intercepted. In March, the Knicks went into a shooting slump and lost 12 of 19 games.

Still, they rallied in April and won their first Atlantic division championship since 1971. Patrick was named NBA Player of the Month. He averaged 24 points, 10.4

rebounds, 3.3 blocks, and 3.4 assists.

Patrick was also busy off the court. He announced he was going into business to produce "Patrick Ewing" sneakers, which he wanted to sell for less than $40 per pair. "I've been bothered by the pressures [the high price of sneakers] have put on our youth," he said. "My mom bought me the only sneakers she could afford and I turned out okay."

The Knicks finished the regular season with 52 wins. Once again they were headed for the playoffs! This time, they hoped to go even farther.

In the first round of the playoffs, the Knicks defeated the Philadelphia 76ers, who were led by forward Charles Barkley. The Knicks advanced to the Eastern Conference semifinal against the Chicago Bulls and their star guard, Michael Jordan.

With former Knick Bill Cartwright at center, the Bulls had become a tough team for the Knicks to beat. Bill was big and strong and was able to move Patrick away from the basket. Michael Jordan took care of everything else. In their best-of-seven series, Michael scored 87 points in two games as the Bulls jumped out to a three games to one lead.

Patrick was criticized in the newspapers for not dominating the games like Michael. Patrick pointed out that he can't control a game because a center doesn't handle the ball as much as a guard like Michael.

In Game 5, Patrick was able to shake free of Bill's defense and score 32 points in a Knick victory. But the Bulls came back to win Game 6 and knock the Knicks out of the playoffs.

The Knicks should have been very happy with their season. But they were hit with a double dose of bad news. Patrick learned he needed surgery to remove loose pieces of cartilage from his knee. Painful knees may have slowed him down in the playoffs, team doctor Norman Scott said, but Patrick would never use that as an excuse.

In addition, Coach Pitino announced he was leaving the Knicks to take a job as head basketball coach at the University of Kentucky. Coach Pitino said he missed working with kids on the college level.

Patrick and the Knick players were disappointed. They had thought they were on the verge of something big. Now they didn't know what it was.

HEAD TO HEAD

In the same season that Patrick led the Knicks to the Eastern Conference semifinals, 1988–89, Alonzo led Georgetown to the Final Eight of the NCAA tournament. That was the closest the Hoyas had come to the NCAA title since Patrick had been their center!

KNOCKED KNICK

That summer, Patrick was treated like a star. He had small roles in two movies, *Exorcist 1990* and *Funny About Love*. He joined Dominique Wilkins and James Worthy to represent the NBA against the winners of a national three-on-three tournament. He was named Player of the Decade by the Big East Conference, which was celebrating its tenth birthday. But Patrick wanted something else: his first NBA championship.

The new head coach of the Knicks was Stu Jackson. Stu was 35 years old, the youngest coach in the league. He had been a Knick assistant coach. Stu wanted the Knicks to take fewer three-point shots and make Patrick the main man in the team's offense.

From the start of the 1989–90 season, Patrick took charge. His scoring average of 29.2 points per game through early December was second in the league. In one game, he scored 44 points and grabbed 24 rebounds, becoming the first Knick to collect more than 20 rebounds in a game since 1971! Patrick was named NBA Player of the Month for November and Player of the Week for the first week in December.

Patrick would come to Knick practices 90 minutes early so he could lift weights. He would even lift on the morning of game days. One writer described Patrick as playing "a season of focused fury."

After posting a 7–5 record in November, the Knicks exploded with an 11–2 run in December. Through mid-January, the team was 26–10, the best record in the Eastern Conference. Patrick was voted to start in the All-Star Game for the first time.

No matter how well Patrick was playing himself, he couldn't do everything on his own. In March, Patrick scored 51 points against the Celtics, but the Knicks lost their sixth straight game anyway. The Knick shooters went cold and New York was 4–12 in March.

Patrick set a new Knick record for scoring in a season with over 2,000 points, but in April the Knicks fell to third place in the Atlantic Division. They stumbled into the playoffs.

And they kept stumbling. The Knicks lost the first two games of their first-round playoff series to the Boston Celtics. In Game 1, the Celtics scored a playoff-record 157 points. Only two teams had ever won a best-of-five playoff series after being down two games to none.

Patrick was angry that the other Knicks had not passed him the basketball more often in Games 1 and 2, and said so. In Game 3, Patrick demanded the ball! He scored 33 points, grabbed 19 rebounds, and led the Knicks to victory. He followed that by scoring 44 points in the Knicks' victory in Game 4, forcing a fifth and deciding game at Boston Garden, where the Knicks had lost 26 straight games. This time, with the Celtics focusing on him, Patrick played smart. He passed the ball well and picked up 10 assists. The Knicks won the game and made history by coming back from two games down!

It was a brief feeling of victory, though. The Knicks were so weary from battling back against the Celtics that in the next playoff round, they folded up against the Detroit Pistons, and lost four games to one.

Still, Patrick did have a great season. In June, he was voted by the media to the all-NBA first team for the first time in his career.

He also had a great off-season. In July, he married Rita Williams, his longtime girlfriend, in a small ceremony at his home in Potomac, Maryland. The couple went to the Caribbean for their honeymoon. But soon Patrick was back working out at the gym at Georgetown. He lifted weights and practiced his passing and rebounding.

When the 1990–91 season got started, the Knicks couldn't seem to get going. They had a record of 7–8 in December. Knick management fired Coach Jackson.

The new coach was John MacLeod, who had been a successful coach with the Phoenix Suns. But the Knicks continued to sink. Their record fell to 14-18 in January and 20–25 in February. One bright spot was that Patrick was named to the All-Star Game, and he scored 18 points, with 10 rebounds and 4 blocks, in the East victory.

Patrick had just about had it with the Knicks. He felt they were getting worse instead of better. He announced he was willing to be traded.

The Knicks barely made the playoffs, and once there, they were embarrassed by the Bulls. The first game, a 126–85 victory by Chicago, was the worst playoff loss in Knick history. The Bulls won three straight games to end the New Yorker's miserable season.

When the season ended, everyone knew it was time for some changes. The team had hired a new president, Dave Checketts, in April, and he had hired Ernie Grunfeld, a former Knick player, to be vice president of player personnel and general manager. Together, they set about to remake the Knicks.

Their first step was to find a new coach. After a long search, the Knicks hired Pat Riley. Coach Riley had coached the Los Angeles Lakers to five NBA championships, and had the best winning percentage as a coach in NBA history.

Their next step was to make sure Patrick was happy. That wouldn't be as easy. Patrick wanted to become a free agent. A section in his contract with the Knicks said that if he was not one of the four highest-paid players in the NBA in his sixth pro year, he could leave the team and go elsewhere. However, because of the complicated way this clause was phrased, it was hard to judge if there were four players in the NBA making more money (as Patrick said) or three (as the Knicks said). Their disagreement had to be settled by an arbitrator, someone who can settle legal arguments outside of a court of law.

Sportswriters wrote that Patrick was being greedy. After all, they said, he was already making over $3 million a season. But Patrick said he was doing it out of principle. He been through six coaches and four general managers in his six years with the Knicks, and wanted the chance to go to a team he felt would try harder to win a championship.

The arbitrator, however, ruled in favor of the Knicks. Patrick said he would honor his contract, but the new Knick management wanted him to know they were committed to winning. They traded for Xavier McDaniel, a rugged, high-scoring forward, and added two talented young players, Anthony Mason and Greg Anthony. Former CBA player John Starks was also becoming an important player for the team. Soon after the season started, the Knicks also gave Patrick a new contract that would pay him an average of $5.4 million a year, making him, at the time, the highest-paid player in team sports.

Patrick had spent the summer, as usual working out hard in the Georgetown gym, with Dikembe Mutombo and Alonzo Mourning. When he arrived at training camp in October, he told reporters he had no bad feelings toward the Knicks, and would work hard as always.

In training camp, Coach Riley worked the players hard so they would be ready to play all-out all season long. They were tired after his practices, but they didn't mind because they felt Coach Riley knew what it takes to build a winning team. Coach Riley realized that Patrick already played hard, but he challenged him to play smarter: to read double teams better, to pass better, to work harder for shots closer to the basket, and to avoid foul trouble.

By January, the Knicks had a record of 22–12 and were leading the Atlantic Division by two games. But once again they slumped down the stretch, and lost the division title to the Celtics. Still, they finished the season second with 51 victories.

In the playoffs, the Knicks defeated the Pistons in the first round and moved on to a rematch with the Chicago Bulls. The Bulls, who had the best record in the league, were expected to win again easily.

But the Knicks were beginning to come together as a team. They won Game 1, 94–89, as Patrick dominated with 34 points, 16 rebounds, 6 blocks and 5 assists.

The series quickly became a war. Players yelled at each other. There was pushing and shoving. Even Patrick and Michael Jordan, friends off the court, got angry with each other in the heat of the games.

The Bulls won Game 5 to take a 3–2 lead. Then, with the score tied in Game 6, Patrick sprained an ankle and had to leave the game. He watched from the bench as the Bulls started to pull away. He couldn't sit and watch his title dreams just disappear. So, with the Madison Square Garden crowd cheering, he went back into the game. Limping up and down the court, Patrick scored 27 points, but mostly he inspired his teammates to win the game, 100-86. It was a great moment for the Knicks!

Game 7 returned the series to Chicago Stadium. This time, the Knicks ran into too much Michael. He scored 42 points, and the Bulls won, 110–81.

Patrick was disappointed, but the season had restored his spirit. "We're a very good ball club," he said. "We can rebound, we can block shots, we can shoot, we can run, and we're going to be good next year."

But for Patrick the basketball year wasn't over yet. He had been selected as a member of the Dream Team, which would represent the United States at the upcoming 1992 Summer Olympic Games in Barcelona, Spain.

HEAD TO HEAD

The same month that Patrick's season ended, June 1992, Alonzo's NBA career began, when he became the second player chosen in the 1992 NBA draft, by the Charlotte Hornets.

PATRICK'S TIME

Imagine a basketball team made up of Patrick Ewing, Michael Jordan, Magic Johnson, Karl Malone, and Charles Barkley. That was the starting five of the 1992 United States Olympic basketball team. David Robinson, John Stockton, and Scottie Pippen would be coming off the bench. No wonder they were called the Dream Team!

This would be the first Olympics in which professional basketball players would be eligible to compete, and Patrick was honored to have been chosen. But soon after the team had begun practicing, Patrick injured his thumb and learned he would have to miss some early games. He didn't let that get him down. He said he would sit on the bench and "be a big cheerleader."

Once they arrived in Barcelona, Spain, for the Olympic Games, the Dream Teamers were treated like rock stars. They couldn't leave the hotel without being mobbed for autographs and their bus needed a police escort to get through the crowds.

The United States team defeated other countries'

teams by as many as 50 points, and easily won the gold medal. Other players seemed honored just to be on the same court with them. Patrick felt he had gotten a lot out of the experience, too. "Anytime you can play with the best, it will make you a better player," he said.

He also became good friends with Larry Bird, the legendary star of the Boston Celtics. He talked to Larry about what it takes to win an NBA title.

At Knick training camp in October 1992, Patrick found a lot of new faces. The Knicks had traded for forward Charles Smith and guards Glen "Doc" Rivers and Rolando Blackman. They had signed free agent veteran center Herb Williams to back up Patrick, and drafted guard Hubert Davis.

Charles, Rolando, and Hubert were good scorers who could take some of the pressure off Patrick. Doc and Herb were clever veterans. The Knicks' goal was more balanced scoring, so they didn't have to depend so heavily on Patrick to score so many points. During the previous year, Patrick's scoring averaged had dropped from 26.6 in 1990-91 to 24 points per game, and the Knicks had won 12 more games.

Patrick also brought something new to camp. Perhaps from talking to the other Dream Teamers, he seemed to have decided to become more of a team leader. Patrick had always led by example, but now he was talking like a leader, too. He urged his teammates to play harder, smarter, and better all the time.

The Knicks started the season with seven new players on their 12-man roster. It took a while for the new players to fit in. The team played inconsistently, sometimes beating a strong team, like the Bulls, then losing to a weaker team, like the Los Angeles Clippers. The Knicks gave up fewer points than any team in the league on defense, but they were second to last in scoring points themselves.

The team was still depending on Patrick to carry the scoring load. But Patrick was tired from having played basketball practically year-round. Plus, he had to face the tough young centers who had just come into the league and wanted to challenge the reigning king of the position.

On November 21, Shaquille O'Neal of the Orlando Magic came to New York. The game was broadcast on national television and an army of sportswriters turned out to see how the 1992 NBA's number one draft pick did in his first test against an All-Star center. Shaquille had 18 points and 17 rebounds to Patrick's 15 points and 9 rebounds, but the Knicks won the game, 92–77.

On December 10, the 1992 NBA number two pick, Patrick's old friend Alonzo Mourning came to New York with his team, the Charlotte Hornets. Patrick had always done well against Charlotte before Alonzo arrived. The Knicks had won eight straight against the Hornets. But the rookie center changed all that. Patrick outscored

Alonzo, 28–22, but Alonzo won the rebounding (17–9) and shot-blocking battles (6–3). More importantly, Alonzo's team won the game.

By February the pieces of the Knick puzzle were beginning to fall into place. Patrick's teammates were playing with the same intensity that he brought to the game. The Knicks had become Patrick's team! The New Yorkers put together a five-game winning streak.

Patrick's game began to come together, too. He was named to the All-Star team for the sixth time in seven years, although he was disappointed that he hadn't been chosen to start. That honor, which was voted by the fans, went to Shaquille O'Neal.

That seemed to spur Patrick to play even harder. In the ten games leading up to the All-Star Game he averaged 27.6 points per game. He was twice named NBA Player of the Week. Right before the All-Star game, he scored 40 points in a game for the 24th time in his career, setting a Knick record.

Patrick continued his fine play after the All-Star break, too. A lot of people were mentioning his name as a serious candidate for Most Valuable Player Award. But Patrick wasn't holding his breath. "I don't know what it is, but I don't get voted into things very often," he said, "but I don't worry about it. My goal is to win a championship."

The Knicks put together a nine-game winning streak in March. They finished the regular season with the best record in the NBA, 60–22.

The Knicks roared into the playoffs. In the first round, they defeated the Indiana Pacers in a best-of-five series, three games to one. Patrick led the Knicks in scoring, with an average of 24.3 points per game. In Game 4, he had 28 points and 13 rebounds in an overtime victory!

The Knicks' second-round opponent was the Charlotte Hornets. That meant another head-to-head matchup between Patrick and Alonzo.

Both centers agreed that their friendship wouldn't get in the way of this being a hard-fought series. "It's always big when two Hoyas get together," Patrick said. "Sure, we're close friends. But we'll save it for the summer. When we get out there, there's no friendship at all."

Patrick and Alonzo even had dinner together before Games 1 and 2 — and then they went to war. In the first game, Patrick scored 33 points, grabbed 10 rebounds, and blocked 4 shots in a Knick victory, while Alonzo had 27 points, 13 rebounds, and 4 blocks. In Game 2, Patrick outscored Alonzo, 34–24, and the Knicks won again.

The Hornets won Game 3 in Charlotte, but in the long run, the Knicks' experience and depth won out. With Patrick topping Alonzo in everything (scoring, rebounding, shooting percentage, and assists) but blocked shots, the Knicks won the series, four games to one.

Coach John Thompson of Georgetown was at most of the games. Before the Series started, he said that he was proud of both players and wished them well, but that "this was Patrick's time."

But it wasn't Patrick's time to win a championship — not yet, anyway. The Knicks' next opponent was the two-time defending NBA champion Chicago Bulls, led by Michael Jordan and Scottie Pippen.

In that series, the Knicks jumped out to a two games to none lead, but then Michael took over. He scored 54 points in Game 4 to even the series at two games apiece.

Patrick gave it his all, averaging nearly 26 points for the series. But the other Knick scorers had gone cold. The Knicks were steamrolled by the Bulls, who won four straight games and ended the Knicks' championship dream once again.

Losing to the Bulls like that was a staggering blow to the Knicks. But, when the 1993–94 season began, Patrick was more determined than ever to make this a championship season for himself and for the Knicks. And with the retirement of Michael Jordan, sportswriters were ready to crown the Knicks NBA champions before the season had even begun.

The Knicks jumped off to a 7–0 start. Patrick scored 32 points and 44 points in the Knicks' first two games. However, nothing is predictable in sports and the team was soon hit by the injury jinx.

First, Patrick went out with a strained neck. When

he returned, he injured his knee. Charles Smith had to miss several weeks to have minor surgery done on his knee, Doc Rivers suffered a leg injury and was lost for the season, and Hubert Davis broke his hand.

Veteran Derek Harper was acquired from Dallas to help out at point guard, but the Knicks floundered through the first half of the season.

But there was a bright side to this dark picture. Although they hadn't played their best, the Knicks still had the third best record in the league, 34–14, at the All-Star break.

In addition, because of all the injuries, a lot of players had gotten a chance to play and to find their shooting touch. So, by the time everyone was healthy, the Knicks were starting to get the kind of balanced scoring they would need if they were going to go all the way to an NBA title.

Patrick himself passed Walt Frazier in the record books to become the Knicks' all-time leading scorer. He also was named to the All-Star Game for the seventh time in his career. Shaquille O'Neal was again voted the starting center, but he had a terrible game, missing his first several shots from the field. Patrick scored 20 points in the East victory, and was the first player to congratulate Shaquille when he made his first shot.

The Knicks finished the regular season with a record of 57–25. Once again, they were champions of the

Atlantic Division. After overcoming so many injuries during the regular season, the Knicks felt that nothing could prevent them from winning the NBA championship. Patrick even told a reporter, "It's our turn to get to the light at the end of the tunnel. This is our year." Patrick wasn't trying to be arrogant; he just wanted to give himself and his teammates a challenge to meet.

Now, it was on to the playoffs!

8
CHAMPIONSHIP DRIVE

NBA players consider the playoffs to be like a second season. The 16 teams (eight in each conference) that make the playoffs all start with a clean slate; it doesn't matter what you did during the regular season.

In the playoffs, two teams play each other in a best-of-five series in the first round, trying to be the first to win three games. The next three rounds are best-of-seven series and teams try to be the first to win four games. The team that wins the series moves on to the next round; the team that loses goes home. A team has to win four series to win the NBA championship.

The Knicks were tied with the Atlanta Hawks for the third-best record in the NBA, behind the Seattle Supersonics and the Houston Rockets. This meant that in the playoffs, the Knicks would have the home-court advantage against teams other than those three. The play-off series would begin on the Knicks' home court and, if the series went the full five or seven games, the last game would be played there, too.

The Knicks began their "second" season by playing their nearby rivals, the New Jersey Nets. The Nets were led by their two All-Stars, point guard Kenny Anderson and power forward Derrick Coleman. The Nets are usually a tough team for the Knicks to beat. Every game between them seems like a battle to see who is the king of basketball in the New York-New Jersey area.

The Nets battled hard but the Knicks' depth and experience were just too much for them to overcome. Led by Patrick's 36 points and 14 rebounds in Game 4, New York won the the best-of-five series, three games to one.

The Knicks' next opponent was the three-time NBA champion Chicago Bulls. In each of the last three years, the Bulls had knocked the Knicks out of the playoffs before going on to win the NBA championship. Would they stop the Knicks again? Even without Michael Jordan, the Bulls were a proud team that played smart basketball. Scottie Pippen, B.J. Armstrong, and Horace Grant were 1994 All-Stars, and Toni Kukoc was a promising rookie who had been a star in Europe.

The Knicks won the first two games of the series, with dramatic fourth-quarter comebacks. But the Bulls bounced back to win Game 3 on a last-second shot by Toni and Game 4 on an outstanding all-around performance by Scottie. This made Knick fans very nervous. Just a year earlier, the Knicks had also won the first two games of their series with the Bulls, only to watch the

Bulls win the next four and the series. Would history repeat itself?

Patrick kept his cool. "Give them credit," he said of the Bulls. "Last year was last year. We just have to regroup, play better than we just did." In a key Game 5, Patrick showed the way. He scored the Knicks' first 6 points, 9 of their first 11, and 14 in the first half. Patrick finished with 20 points and 13 rebounds, leading the Knicks to an 87–86 victory. Although the Bulls won Game 6, the Knicks finished them off at Madison Square Garden in Game 7. The Knicks had finally beaten the Bulls to move on to the Eastern Conference Finals.

The Knicks' path to the NBA Finals still wasn't going to be easy. It ran through the Indiana Pacers. The Pacers had had a great second half of the season, and had upset the Orlando Magic and Atlanta Hawks to get this far. They had an oustanding shooting guard in Reggie Miller, plus they had been playing the same kind of tough defense that the Knicks were famous for.

Once again, the Knicks won the first two games of the series at Madison Square Garden, but the Pacers won the next two games on *their* home court. The Knicks were confident returning to play Game 5 at the Garden, but they were in for a shock. With the Knicks leading in the fourth quarter, Reggie Miller caught fire. Reggie couldn't miss a shot and exploded for 25 points in the fourth quarter alone, outscoring the entire Knick team for the period!

The Pacers won, 93–86, and took a 3–2 lead in the series. They would be going home to Indiana with a chance to win the series.

All of a sudden, the Knicks had their backs against the wall: They were one game away from being eliminated from the playoffs. But they battled back to win Game 6. Now the Knicks would have to play Game 7 at Madison Square Garden, another do-or-die contest.

Patrick had his best game of the playoffs, as he contributed 24 points, 22 rebounds, 7 assists, and 5 blocked shots. Still, the game came down to the final seconds. With the Knicks down by one point and just 35 seconds left to play, Patrick set a screen for Knick guard John Starks. John drove to the basket and reached up around some Pacers for a layup. Patrick moved close to the basket. When John's layup came off the front rim, Patrick leapt high into the air, grabbed the ball with both hands, and slammed it into the basket. The Knicks had won. For the first time since Patrick had joined the team, the Knicks were going to the NBA Finals!

"I looked up, and there was Patrick coming out of the sky," said John after the game. "You can't say enough about Patrick. He wanted this. He deserved this, to get to the point in his career to have a chance to play for the championship. And Big Fella wasn't going to let us lose."

Even the Pacers were happy for Patrick. "If anybody in this league deserves a chance, it's him," said

Pacer backup center Lasalle Thompson. "He's a true warrior. He plays hard every night. *Every* night."

That would be Patrick's best game of the playoffs. The Knicks' opponent in the Finals was the Houston Rockets, who were led by center Hakeem Olajuwon. For the regular season, Hakeem had been named the league's Defensive Player of the Year and its Most Valuable Player.

Hakeem, like Patrick, was born outside of the United States, in Nigeria, and did not play basketball until he was a teenager. In college, the 7' center had led the University of Houston to two appearances in the NCAA championship game. In 1984, he and Patrick had played against each other for the NCAA title. Patrick's Georgetown team had won.

The Rockets were favored to win the series. They had beaten the Knicks in both of their regular season games, and they had the home-court advantage because they had a better regular season record. They also had three dangerous outside shooters in Vernon Maxwell, Robert Horry, and Kenny Smith, and a rugged rebounding forward in Otis Thorpe.

But the Knicks were battlers, and the series would be the closest Finals in NBA history, with no team winning a game by more than nine points. "If Houston is the favorite, fine," said Patrick. "We don't care about that. The fact is, we're here. A lot of people counted us out and we're here."

The Rockets won the first game, at The Summit, their home arena, but the Knicks came back to win Game 2. The series moved to New York, where the Rockets won Game 3. Then, behind fine shooting by guards John Starks and Derrick Harper, the Knicks won Games 4 and 5, to take a 3–2 edge in the series.

Patrick wasn't shooting well but he made up for it with his defense. He had six blocked shots in Game 2, seven in Game 3 (with 13 rebounds), and eight in Game 5. For the series, he would block 30 shots, a playoff record. He was cheered on at Madison Square Garden by John Thompson, Alonzo Mourning, and Dikembe Mutombo.

The series moved back to Houston, and the Knicks just had to win one of two games to be NBA champions. But the Rockets would not go down easily. The Knicks had their best chance in Game 6, but a last second shot by John Starks that would have won the game was deflected by Hakeem.

Now it all came down to one game to decide the NBA title. It would also be played on the Rockets' home court. In recent NBA playoff history, the home team had won the previous 19 Game 7's.

The Knicks battled hard, but their shots were not going in. They were playing in their 25th playoff game and their 115th game of the season (including preseason), the most in NBA history, and they seemed tired from the long war. They were down by just three points with less than seven minutes to play, but they just couldn't catch the Rockets. Led by Hakeem's 25 points and 10 rebounds, the Rockets won the game — and the NBA title — 90–84. Hakeem was named the MVP of the series. Patrick would have to wait another season to try for that elusive NBA championship.

Patrick was very disappointed to have come so close and come up short. "It hurts, period," he said. Then he added, "I'm still very proud and I have a lot of pride in my teammates."

It had been a great battle between two great centers. After the game, Hakeem came over to give Patrick a hug. "I told him, hopefully maybe next year," he said. "He deserves it. If anybody deserves it, Patrick deserves to win."

Coach Riley added a few words of his own. "I've never been around a guy more committed to making his team work," he said of Patrick. "He's a true warrior. He will bounce back . . . he will be back."

* * *

Patrick is dedicated to his profession. Before games, you can find him sitting quietly at his locker, listening to reggae or jazz on his headphones while intently watching game tapes of that night's opponent. After games, he is back in his chair, holding bags of ice against his knees to relieve the pain and politely answering reporter's questions. In between, he steps onto the basketball court and gives his team everything he has.

Patrick has never wanted to be an NBA celebrity like Shaquille or Michael or Charles Barkley. Off the court, his favorite things to do are just to spend time with friends and family — his wife Rita, his 9-year old son Patrick, Jr. and his 2-year-old daughter Randi — listen to music, tinker with his cars, and work out.

"He doesn't want people to know him," says Doc Rivers, "just to accept him as a great player."

All his life, Patrick has heard people tell him what he couldn't do, and then he has gone out and done it. They said he couldn't read, but he graduated from college and started his own business. They said he couldn't play basketball, but he became one of the greatest centers in NBA history. They said he was a cold-hearted loner, but he has grown into a man who gives a lot of himself to his community.

Many great players never get the opportunity to win an NBA championship. It takes the right combination of teammates and luck. But, no matter what he does in the rest of his basketball career, Patrick Ewing is already a champion — on the court and off.

PATRICK EWING'S CAREER STATS

COLLEGE STATS
Georgetown University

SEASONS	Games	POINTS Total	POINTS Avg	REBOUNDS Total	REBOUNDS Avg.	BLKS Total	BLKS Avg.
1981-82	37	469	12.7	279	7.5	119	3.2
1982-83	32	565	17.7	325	10.2	106	3.3
1983-84	37	608	16.4	371	10.0	133	3.6
1984-85	37	542	14.6	341	9.2	135	3.6
Totals	143	2,184	15.3	1,316	9.2	493	3.4

PRO STATS
New York Knicks

SEASONS	Games	POINTS Total	POINTS Avg.	REBOUNDS Total	REBOUNDS Avg.	BLKS Total	BLKS Avg.
1985-86	50	998	20.0	451	9.0	103	2.0
1986-87	63	1356	21.5	555	8.8	147	2.3
1987-88	82	1653	20.2	676	8.2	245	2.9
1988-89	80	1815	22.7	740	9.2	281	3.5
1989-90	82	2347	28.6	893	10.9	327	3.9
1990-91	81	2154	26.6	905	11.2	258	3.1
1991-92	82	1970	24.0	921	11.2	245	2.9
1992-93	81	1959	24.2	980	12.0	161	1.9
1993-94	79	1939	24.5	885	11.2	217	2.7
Totals	601	14,252	23.7	6,121	9.5	1,984	2.8

Patrick (here with Coach Mike Jarvis) led his high school team to a record of 77-1 and three Massachusetts state championships!

In his four years at Georgetown University, Patrick guided the Hoyas to the NCAA basketball finals three times and to the national championship in 1984.

Les Kimbrough

Noren Trotman/Sports Photo Masters

Patrick was known at Georgetown for his defense, but he has become one of the best shooting big men in NBA history.

Alonzo was known for his shotblocking in college, but he has averaged more than 20 points a game as a center for the Charlotte Hornets.

Tim O'Dell

Tim O'Dell

PATRICK GOT HIS NICKNAME "BEAST OF THE EAST" AT GEORGETOWN UNIVERSITY FOR HIS GREAT DEFENSE...

"A TOUGH LOSS FOR GEORGETOWN AS THE TAR HEELS WIN THE NATIONAL TITLE, 63-62..."

THAT PATRICK EWING IS A SUPER PLAYER... I WANT TO BE LIKE HIM SOMEDAY!

ALONZO BEGAN PRACTICING BASKETBALL EVERY DAY AFTER SCHOOL. AT FIRST, HE WASN'T VERY GOOD AND GOT TEASED BY OTHER KIDS...

ALONZO MAY BE TALL — BUT HE STINKS !!!

PATRICK GRADUATED FROM *GEORGETOWN* IN 1985 AND WAS THE #1 DRAFT PICK FOR *THE NEW YORK KNICKS*...

ALONZO WAS NAMED THE *TOP 11TH GRADE PLAYER* IN THE NATION, AND HIS HIGH SCHOOL TEAM WON THE STATE CHAMPIONSHIP...

ALONZO'S AWESOME!!!

HE'S BEEN RECRUITED BY MORE THAN *100* COLLEGES !!!

PATRICK AND *ALONZO* MET AT A BASKETBALL CAMP IN *PRINCETON, NEW JERSEY*...

WOW! IT'S REALLY *HIM*!

PATRICK WAS SELECTED FOR THE "**DREAM TEAM**" THAT REPRESENTED THE **U.S.** AT THE 1992 SUMMER OLYMPICS. WITH OTHER STARS LIKE **MICHAEL JORDAN** AND **MAGIC JOHNSON**, THE AMERICANS CRUSHED THEIR OPPONENTS TO BRING HOME THE GOLD...

NOBODY CAN TOUCH THESE GUYS!

ALONZO GRADUATED FROM **GEORGETOWN** AND WAS THE **#2** PICK IN THE **NBA** DRAFT BY THE **CHARLOTTE HORNETS** ...

19

AFTER THE OLYMPICS, **PATRICK, ALONZO** AND **DIKEMBE MUTOMBO** MET FOR THEIR SUMMER WORKOUT AT THE **GEORGETOWN GYM**...

TRY THAT IN **CHARLOTTE** NEXT SEASON!

ALONZO AND PATRICK FINALLY PLAYED THEIR FIRST **NBA** GAME AGAINST EACH OTHER IN DECEMBER 1992. THOUGH PATRICK OUTSCORED ALONZO 28-22, ALONZO GRABBED 17 REBOUNDS AND LED THE **HORNETS** TO A 110-103 UPSET VICTORY OVER THE **KNICKS** ...

IF WE CAN'T WIN, I HOPE YOU GUYS GO ALL THE WAY!

CHARLOTTE AND **NEW YORK** MET IN THE SECOND ROUND OF THE '93 PLAYOFFS. ALONZO AND THE **HORNETS** BATTLED HARD AGAINST PATRICK AND THE **KNICKS**, BUT NEW YORK WENT ON TO WIN 3 GAMES TO 1.

PATRICK AND ALONZO MAY NOT BE BUDDIES AT GAME TIME BUT OFF THE COURT THEY HAVE A SPECIAL FRIENDSHIP!

Alonzo led Indian River High School to a 1987 Virginia state champion- ship and was one of the top high school players in the country.

Alonzo wore Patrick's number at Georgetown but had his own aggressive style on the court.

Manny Millan/Sports Illustrated

During NBA off-seasons, Alonzo and Patrick still work on their games together at the Georgetown University gym.

No matter how heated their one-on-one battles get, Patrick and Alonzo are still friends after the buzzer sounds.

Tim O'Dell

TIMEOUT!

HEADS UP, HOOPS FANS.

HEAD-TO-HEAD BASKETBALL is a very different kind of book; it can be read frontwards or backwards. Start from one end and you'll get the inside stuff on the New York Knicks' all-star center, Patrick Ewing. Or start from the other side to get the lowdown on the Charlotte Hornets' big man, Alonzo Mourning.

Whichever way you begin, you'll want to read *both* superstar stories *before* jumping into the amazing middle section of the book. Read how Patrick and Alonzo battle on the court — but remain great friends off it — *then* check out the fantastic photos, stats, and comic strip that shows just how these two NBA giants stack up against each other.

Ok, it's tip-off time. So pick Alonzo or Patrick and get ready for all the Head-to-Head action!

ALONZO MOURNING

by Neil Cohen

A Sports Illustrated For Kids Book

Bantam Books

NEW YORK • TORONTO • LONDON • SYDNEY • AUCKLAND

CONTENTS

THE STUDENT VS. THE TEACHER

Alonzo Mourning should have been nervous. There he was, a rookie center in the National Basketball Association (NBA), at Madison Square Garden in New York City, about to play his first pro game against his idol, Patrick Ewing of the New York Knicks.

Alonzo had idolized Patrick since he was a kid and had seen Patrick play on TV for Georgetown University. Later on, Patrick had helped convince Alonzo that he should attend Georgetown University, too.

Even though Alonzo was eight years younger than Patrick, they had become friends During summers, they worked out together at the Georgetown University gym. They talked on the phone often and had dinner together when they were in the same city.

Alonzo, 22 years old, had played well so far in his rookie season, averaging 17 points and 9 rebounds a game. So had the Hornets, who were 9–9 in only their

fifth season in the NBA. But now, on December 10, 1992, Alonzo and the Hornets were facing a big test. The Knicks were one of the best teams in the league. The main reason for that was Patrick.

Patrick was a seven-time All-Star center. He had averaged more than 23 points and almost 10 rebounds per game in his seven seasons with New York. In two games versus Charlotte earlier that season, Patrick had ripped the Hornets for 45 and 40 points. So far, the Knicks were 11–6, and they had beaten the Hornets the last eight times the two teams met.

Patrick and Alonzo had looked forward to this game. They had talked about it at their Georgetown workouts. As Alonzo and his teammates took the court, Hornet coach Allan Bristow expected Alonzo to be a little uptight.

"I figured he'd be a little hyper because of the Patrick Ewing matchup," said Coach Bristow, "but he probably was as collected as he's been."

Patrick and Alonzo shook hands at center court when they met for the jump ball to start the game. But that's where the politeness ended.

The first time Alonzo got the ball on offense, he turned on Patrick and tried a quick jump shot from close to the basket. *Swat!* Patrick blocked the shot and the ball went sailing out of bounds. When the ball was passed back in to Alonzo, he tried a long jump shot from the corner. *Slam!* Patrick swatted that one away, too.

Another rookie might have gotten discouraged, but not Alonzo. "That wasn't the first time he's blocked my shots," Alonzo said later, "so I wasn't surprised. Patrick's a great player, an All-Star. He's supposed to block shots."

The Knicks took the early lead. They were ahead, 28–23, after the first quarter, and 51–43 at halftime.

But the Hornets stayed in the game. In the head-to-head matchup of centers, Patrick was the polished veteran, scoring on jump shots and drives to the basket. Alonzo was the rookie, missing many of his shots and turning the ball over. But Alonzo battled for every rebound and contested every shot.

The two big men also talked some trash. "We kidded each other on the court," said Alonzo. "He knows what I like to do. I know what he likes to do."

Charlotte came on strong in the third quarter, and took the lead, 76–69. The Knicks tied the score with seconds remaining in the game. When New York missed a shot at the buzzer, the game went into overtime.

The Knicks scored the first basket in the extra period, but then the Hornets took over, scoring the next 11 points. Led by Alonzo's defense, the Hornets held the Knicks to just two points in the first three minutes of the overtime. The Hornets pulled away and won the game, 110–103. The first pro matchup between Alonzo and Patrick had gone to the new kid's team!

Patrick had 28 points, 9 rebounds, and 3 blocked

shots. Alonzo scored 22 points, grabbed 17 rebounds, and blocked 6 shots. Alonzo made only 7 of 19 shots and committed 6 turnovers — but all in all, the student did very well in his first game against the teacher.

"He didn't shoot well, but he did all the other things," said Patrick after the game.

"We got out-hustled tonight," said Knick guard Doc Rivers. "Alonzo Mourning was running up and down the court creating havoc like a crazy man."

Everyone agreed that with Alonzo at center, the Hornets were not just a lowly expansion club anymore, but a team that would battle hard in every game.

As reporters gathered around to ask him questions about this big victory, Alonzo was calm and low-key. He talked about how the team had played, not about himself. "Defense was the biggest factor in this game," he said. "We shut them down, made them take bad shots."

As for his matchup with Patrick, Alonzo said it was just his night this time. "We both realize that anybody in this league can get beat on any given night," he said.

Alonzo knew better than to get too excited. After a bumpy ride through the first 22 years of his life, he was happy to just enjoy the fact that he had finally arrived in the NBA.

FROM STUMBLER TO STAR

Alonzo Mourning, Jr., was born in Chesapeake, Virginia, on February 8, 1970. Chesapeake is a city of more 175,00 people in southeastern Virginia, near where the James River empties into Chesapeake Bay.

When Alonzo was 12 years old, his parents — Alonzo Sr. and Julia — were divorced. Alonzo was given the choice of living with his mother or his father. Instead, he chose to move into the home of Fannie Threet, a family friend. Ms. Threet and her husband had two kids, but she had also helped to raise many foster children.

"I wasn't mad at [my parents]," Alonzo remembers, "but I wasn't comfortable at home. Divorce is hard to understand when you're a kid."

Alonzo lived with the Threets for the next eight years. Ms. Threet treated Alonzo like one of her own children, even though there were often as many as nine other foster kids living in the house. She encouraged Alonzo to

set goals for himself and made sure he worked hard in school. "Fannie guided me every step of the way," Alonzo says. "Her message was always: You can do it."

When Alonzo was 12, he was already 6' 3 1/2" tall. But he didn't play basketball. That year, 1982, he watched the National Collegiate Athletic Association (NCAA) men's basketball championship game on TV. The game was between the University of North Carolina Tar Heels and the Georgetown University Hoyas. The Tar Heels won, but Alonzo liked the way Georgetown's freshman center played. His name was Patrick Ewing.

"That game inspired me to go out and play basketball," says Alonzo. "I had been more into football, but I went out the next day and bought a Georgetown T-shirt with the money I had made cutting grass."

Ms. Threet had a family friend put up a backboard and a basket in the field across the street from her house. Alonzo began playing and practicing basketball whenever he wasn't in school or doing his homework.

He had difficulty with basketball at first. The kids he played with used to make fun of him. They didn't think he would ever be any good at the game.

"People expected me to be good because I was [tall]," Alonzo remembers. "I was taller than the principal in my school. But I was very awkward and clumsy. People kidded me about the way I played. I would get embarrassed because I would slip and fall." That just made

Alonzo want to work harder, to prove that the people who underestimated him were wrong.

When Ms. Threet saw how hard Alonzo was practicing and how serious he was about playing basketball, she arranged for Alonzo to attend summer basketball camps. Alonzo attended basketball camp beginning with the summer of 1982, before his first year in junior high school, and for several summers afterward.

"That helped me a lot because of the competition and trying to match myself against the best players in camp," Alonzo says. "I was young, but I tried to play against the older guys."

As a result, his play improved by leaps and bounds. Alonzo played on his junior high school team. He got better *and* bigger. Alonzo had a huge appetite. "I'll go to the grocery store and buy five or six boxes of Cap'n Crunch [cereal], expecting them to last several weeks," said Ms. Threet. "He'll sit down and eat two boxes for breakfast."

Alonzo was also becoming a fierce competitor who didn't take losing lightly. He didn't believe in the saying, "You win some, you lose some." After a loss, he was so upset that he would go home and go right to bed.

By the fall of 1984, when he began attending Indian River High School in Chesapeake, Alonzo had grown to be 6' 9" tall. He wore number 33, the same number as his two favorite players: Patrick Ewing and Kareem Abdul-Jabbar. He hung a picture of Patrick on his bedroom wall.

In the summer of 1985, when Alonzo was 15, he was invited to the Five Star Basketball Camp in Pittsburgh, Pennsylvania, one of the top basketball camps for high school players. The best players in the country are invited to display their talent for college coaches. Coaches who had only heard about Alonzo didn't expect him to really be as good as people said. But he was. Camp director Howard Garfinkel remembers thinking Alonzo was the best he'd seen at that age since Lew Alcindor (later called Kareem Abdul-Jabbar).

By the start of his junior year, Alonzo was rated the best 11th-grade basketball player in the nation by *Sports Illustrated*. Alonzo backed that up by averaging 21 points, 11 rebounds, and 9.6 blocked shots per game. He led Indian River to a 29–1 record and the state championship! Alonzo was named a high school All-America.

He could have scored more points that season, but he was not interested in that. "Alonzo's the type of person who doesn't care about the number of points," said his coach, Bill Lassiter. "If his team wins, he wins."

Ms. Threet never went to Alonzo's basketball games, but she helped him with his schoolwork whenever he asked. Coach Lassiter reminded Alonzo that to be eligible to play basketball as a college freshman he needed a 2.0 grade point average and at least a score of 700 on the Scholastic Aptitude Test (SAT), which is a college entrance exam.

In June of that year, Alonzo took the SATs and failed to get the 700 score. Alonzo said he had not studied for the test at all. Coach Lassiter thought Alonzo had let all the basketball praise he was getting go to his head. "If you feel very important in one aspect of your life, then something [else] is going to go lagging," he explained.

That summer, Alonzo traveled with the Virginia Amateur Athletic Union (AAU) team to tournaments in Jacksonville, Florida; Los Angeles, California; and Las Vegas, Nevada. In one game, Alonzo blocked 27 shots.

During that same summer, Alonzo also attended a basketball camp in Princeton, New Jersey. That's where he first met Patrick Ewing, who was by then a member of the New York Knicks. "He came up to me and shook my hand," Alonzo remembers. "It was a big thrill."

Back home in the fall, Alonzo started looking for a college. Over 100 schools offered him an athletic scholarships. Alonzo narrowed down the choices to Maryland, Virginia, Syracuse, Georgia Tech, and Georgetown.

He invited each of the school's coaches to visit him at home and talk to him and his parents. (Even though he had lived with Fannie Threet most of his teenage years, Alonzo still relied on his parents for advice and support.) He also visited the college campuses. Under NCAA rules, he could make one all-expenses-paid visit to each school.

Campus visits sometimes turn out to be whirlwind weekends, with parties, concerts, visits to clubs, and stays

in fancy hotels. But not at Georgetown. There Alonzo stayed in the dormitory with the members of the basketball team, ate pizza, went to one party, and ate brunch the next morning with coach John Thompson and the team's academic counselor to talk about his education.

Alonzo announced in November 1987 that he would be going to Georgetown. He took the SATs again, after studying for them. This time he scored a passing grade.

In his senior year, Alonzo averaged 24.5 points, 15 rebounds, and 10 blocked shots per game, and led Indian River to a 28–2 record and to the semifinals of the state tournament. He was named Gatorade National Basketball Player of the Year. In just six years, Alonzo, now 18, had gone from a clumsy kid to the best high school player in the country. And now he was off to follow in the footsteps of his hero, Patrick Ewing, at Georgetown.

"He's not going to make them forget Ewing," said a college coach who had seen Alonzo, "but he's going to be right there doing everything Ewing did."

HEAD TO HEAD

When Alonzo was 15 years old, Patrick was playing his first season with the New York Knicks and was named NBA Rookie of the Year.

FAB
FRESHMAN

Before Alonzo left for Georgetown, he had another basketball adventure: He was invited to try out for the 1988 United States Olympic basketball team.

Other high school seniors had been invited to try out for the Olympic team in the past, but none had ever made the squad. Alonzo was determined not to be intimidated by competing for a spot against such great college players as Danny Manning and David Robinson. "They haven't done anything I'm not capable of doing," he said.

The coach of the Olympic team was Georgetown coach John Thompson. Some people whispered that Alonzo had been invited to the Olympic Trials only because of Coach Thompson. But Alonzo soon proved that he belonged there.

"He has the maturity of a [college] sophomore," said Dwayne Schintzius, a 7-foot center from the University of Florida, after seeing Alonzo play. "At his stage, a lot of guys are tall, but tall and skinny. I was scared to take the ball to the basket. This guy will take the

ball to the hole and knock your teeth out."

Alonzo almost made the Olympic team. He was the second-to-last player cut. He was disappointed, but he felt he'd gotten a head start on his college basketball career.

The freshman class that started college in the fall of 1988 featured several promising players, including Christian Laettner of Duke, LaPhonso Ellis of Notre Dame, and Billy Owens of Syracuse. But no freshman got more attention than Alonzo.

Sportswriters expected Alonzo to help the Hoyas play the way they had in the early 1980's, when Patrick Ewing led them to three NCAA finals and one national championship. With Alonzo at center, they wrote, the Hoyas could play the kind of tough defense they had played with Patrick. Alonzo was also expected to be a better offensive player than Patrick had been as a freshman.

Alonzo asked for and was given Patrick's uniform number, 33. But Coach Thompson discouraged comparisons between the two centers. "Alonzo's going to be a fine player," he said. "But he doesn't have to be Patrick; he just has to be Alonzo. "

Alonzo felt the same way. "It's going to be hard to follow in Patrick's footsteps because he's done so much for Georgetown," he said. "That's why I have to make my own path and do something different from what he did."

Alonzo began doing that right away. In the Hoyas' very first home game, in December, a victory over St. Leo

College, Alonzo scored 11 points, grabbed 10 rebounds, and blocked 11 shots. He recorded the school's first triple-double (reaching double figures in three categories) since John Thompson became coach in 1972. His 11 blocks broke Patrick's single-game Georgetown record.

Sportswriters had to keep reminding their readers that Alonzo was still only 18 and just a freshman, but Alonzo seemed to have that in perspective. "I know that I'm human," he said, "and I know that I'm not going to go out and score, like, 50 points every game."

Whenever Alonzo let the attention distract him, Coach Thompson set him straight. One time, Alonzo wasn't taking schoolwork seriously. Coach Thompson sat him down and asked him to imagine that he had become what he always dreamed of being, the most dominant force in the NBA. "What if you found out then — and only then," asked Coach, "that you had a mind? That God had also given you — and only you — the gift to cure cancer? Would that bother you?" That got Alonzo to study harder.

On the court, Alonzo was awesome. Against the University of Miami, he scored 26 points and grabbed 17 rebounds. In a game with the University of Pittsburgh, he had 15 points and 7 blocks.

Hoya guard Charles Smith, who had played with Patrick Ewing, said if Alonzo kept improving, he would be every bit as good as Patrick.

Actually, Alonzo was already doing a little better.

After his first 18 games, Patrick's Georgetown team was 14–4; Alonzo's Georgetown team was 16–2. At that point in his freshman year, Patrick was averaging 12.4 points per game on almost 66 percent shooting, with 135 rebounds, 16 assists, and 65 blocks. Alonzo was averaging 13.2 points on 65 percent shooting, with 147 rebounds, 20 assists, and 99 blocks.

Alonzo still made freshman mistakes, but as Coach Thompson said, "He's still a freshman. Shot selection. Impatience. But he makes sins of commission rather than omission. I think that's good. And his work habits are as good as Patrick's."

Alonzo seemed to be having more fun than Patrick did when he was at Georgetown. Patrick had always been very serious on the court. Alonzo would raise his fist after a good play and sometimes joke around with the fans. At Georgetown home games in the Capital Centre, fans set up a cheering section for Alonzo called "Rejection Row." Every time he blocked a shot, they held up cards with a hand drawn on them.

Alonzo was also getting some help from teammate Dikembe Mutombo. Dikembe was a 7' 4" sophomore from Zaire, Africa. He was still learning the game, but he was talented. That season, Dikembe broke Alonzo's record by blocking 12 shots in a game.

The Hoyas finished the regular season with a 23–4 record and were ranked Number 3 in the country. Alonzo

was named Big East Defensive Player of the Year. He led the nation in blocked shots with 135 in 27 games (an average of 5 per game), which tied Patrick's freshman record. He led the Hoyas in rebounding with 7.4 per game and in field goal percentage, .598. With Alonzo and Dikembe, the Hoyas set an NCAA single-season team record with 309 blocked shots.

In the Big East tournament at Madison Square Garden, Georgetown cruised to an 82–52 victory over Boston College in the quarterfinals. Alonzo had eight blocked shots, breaking a tournament record.

The Hoyas defeated Pittsburgh, 85–62, in the semifinal game and advanced to the conference finals against Syracuse and its star, Derrick Coleman. Alonzo had a great game, with 21 points and 4 blocked shots to lead Georgetown to an 88–79 victory and the Big East title.

Patrick Ewing was at that game. He and Alonzo had kept in touch after their first meeting and would often talk on the telephone. After the game, Patrick went down to the tunnel between the court and the lockerroom to give Alonzo a high-five.

Some people were now predicting that the Hoyas would win the 1989 NCAA tournament. But Georgetown nearly lost in its first-round game against Princeton University, a team the Hoyas were favored to beat. Georgetown needed two blocked shots by Alonzo in the final seconds to hold on to the victory.

The Hoyas defeated North Carolina State to reach the Final Eight of the tournament, but they would have to beat Duke University to get to the Final Four. Patrick had taken Georgetown to the Final Four in *his* freshman year.

The game against Duke matched Alonzo against Duke's freshman center Christian Laettner, whom Alonzo had outplayed in high school all-star games. But this time it was Christian who dominated. Christian scored 24 points and grabbed 9 rebounds, while holding Alonzo to 11 points and 5 rebounds. Duke went to the Final Four and Georgetown went home.

It was a disappointing ending, but Alonzo was upbeat about his freshman year. "My attitude is great toward learning," he said. "If I keep growing, maturing, and learning, there's no telling how good I can get."

Little did Alonzo know that this would be the closest he would ever come to a college championship.

HEAD TO HEAD

Although Alonzo didn't make the 1988 U.S. Olympic team, he played on Dream Team II, the U.S. team at the 1994 world championships. Patrick played on the 1984 and 1992 U.S. Olympic teams, and won two gold medals!

SLAM-DUNKED!

Alonzo spent much of the summer of 1989 working on his game. A righthanded shooter, he added a lefthanded hook shot to keep defensive players guessing. He also lifted weights with Dikembe. That fall, Coach Thompson was impressed by how strong Alonzo had become. In practices, he said, "I see my players jumping out of his way."

But before the season started, Alonzo himself had a frightening experience. He was called to testify at the trial of a man named Rayful Edmond III and 10 other people. Edmond was charged with the crime of selling the drug crack cocaine. Alonzo had been introduced to Edmond by a former Hoya teammate. Alonzo said he didn't know that Edmond was a drug dealer.

Alonzo testified for more than an hour in a courtroom shielded by bullet-proof glass. He told the judge and jury that he had visited Edmond and another defendant at their homes to watch sports events on TV, but had never seen drugs, drug materials, or large amounts of cash

around the houses. He said he had stopped seeing them after Coach Thompson had warned the team about Edmond's criminal reputation.

Alonzo was shaken by the experience. He had learned that many people will want to hang out with him because he is a famous athlete, but that he has to be careful of how he chooses his friends. "I made a mistake and I have to learn from the mistake," he said.

Soon Alonzo was able to concentrate on basketball again. Coach Thompson had decided to play Alonzo and Dikembe together in the lineup more often. At those times, Dikembe, at 7' 4" would be the center, and Alonzo, at 6' 10", would be the power forward.

The Alonzo and Dikembe Show got off to a very good start. Through Georgetown's first 17 games, Dikembe blocked 73 shots and Alonzo blocked 41.

Alonzo was the team's leading scorer. He was averaging 18 points per game and connecting on 18-foot jump shots, now that he was free to roam the court as a power forward. In a game against Virginia Tech just before Christmas, Alonzo scored a career-high 27 points.

However, as the season moved through January and into February, Alonzo fell into a deep shooting slump and Georgetown lost some big games. Because he was the best scorer on the team, Alonzo was getting double- and triple-teamed by opposing defenses.

Alonzo got frustrated. He began talking trash to

other players on the floor and sometimes trying to bully them. "He tries to get you going with a lot of rah-rah and throwing elbows," said St. John's forward Malik Sealy. But his trash talk only made other players more revved up to face him. "With Mourning, it's enough incentive to just be playing against him," said Providence forward Marty Conlon. "For him to do that kind of stuff — wow! — it gets under your skin and makes you want to play even better."

In a game with the University of Connecticut, Alonzo lined up for a free throw next to Nadav Henefeld, a forward who came from Israel, and reportedly gave him an earful of ethnic insults. Nadav dismissed the whole thing as "just something that happens in a basketball game." The next time the two teams played, Nadav said, Alonzo came over and said he was sorry.

Alonzo finished the season second on the team in scoring (16.5 per game), rebounding (8.5), and blocked shots (69). It was a disappointing season for the Hoyas. In the NCAA tournament, they were upset in the first round by tiny Xavier College.

During the summer, Alonzo was co-captain of the United States team that played in the Goodwill Games and the World Championships. However, during the competition, Alonzo suffered a strained arch in his left foot, an injury that would continue to bother him later.

In his junior season, Alonzo was expected to be one of the leaders of a young Hoya team. There were six

freshmen and a transfer student on the roster.

Dikembe, the only senior, was named team captain. Coach Thompson decided to give Dikembe more playing time at center so that he would be able to prove himself to the NBA scouts. Alonzo found himself mostly playing power forward. Coach Thompson felt this would be good experience because he thought Alonzo would probably play power forward in the NBA.

Alonzo was happy to learn another position on the floor, but he still saw himself as a center. "I also know where I'm most comfortable: in the paint, drawing fouls, getting hit upside the head, and going to the foul line where I have 10 free seconds to concentrate and hit foul shots with nobody standing in front of me," he said. "A big, strong person ought to be able to do that."

Still, Alonzo did not complain about playing forward. He and Dikembe were good friends, who helped each other in practice and on the court.

In an early December game against Duke, Alonzo showed that he could still take over a game. He dominated from the start. In one series, Alonzo dunked off an offensive rebound to tie the game at 10. Then, he dunked-off another offensive rebound to put the Hoyas ahead, 12–10. He hit an 18-foot jump shot to make it 16–10 and stuck back another offensive rebound to make it 18–10. Duke battled back, and the score was close the whole game. The Blue Devils had a chance to tie the game with

about 12 seconds left. But Alonzo swatted away an inside shot to end the game and give the Hoyas the victory. He finished with 22 points, 10 rebounds, 4 blocks, and 2 steals.

But that great game had a down side. On the game-saving block, Alonzo reinjured the arch of his left foot. He had to sit out most of the next six weeks, missing 9 of 10 games and playing in only parts of others.

Even after he rejoined the Hoyas in mid-January, Alonzo was unable to get back in sync with the team. His shooting was rusty and he couldn't seem to get comfortable on the court. The Hoyas were losing games they should have been winning, and some sportswriters were criticizing Alonzo for not being the next Patrick Ewing after all.

Patrick himself came to Alonzo's defense in the newspapers. He knew that a lot of people had forgotten how long it had taken him to mature as a basketball player, and that, even now as a member of the Knicks, he was still developing.

"People won't realize how good Alonzo can be until he gets to the pros," Patrick said. "A lot of that has to do with the way defenses play, the way the college game is played differently from the pros, the way big guys sometimes need more time to grow, to mature. I'm telling you, a lot of what's happening to him reminds me of me. All he needs to do is keep his head and keep playing hard."

The Hoyas often played their home games at the Capital Centre (now called the USAir Arena), the home arena of the Washington Bullets. One day in late February, after a Knicks-Bullets game at the Centre, Patrick left a message for the Hoyas, who would be playing Connecticut there that night. On the blackboard he wrote "Good Luck," and drew a smiling face. That night, Alonzo responded with his first big game since the Duke contest. He scored 20 points, grabbed 13 rebounds, and blocked 4 shots in a 71–57 win.

"It's been real hard," Alonzo said, referring to the season. "The way people play me, injuries, going through slumps, not playing up to your own expectations, it's all part of growing up and maturing. Like any young player, I'm learning, falling down and getting up again. . . . But this game, hopefully, is a great start for me."

The Hoyas finished the regular season with a 16–11 record and an 8–8 mark in the Big East, their worst record since joining the conference 12 years earlier. But Alonzo's late season play gave them reason to hope. In the final game of the regular season, a loss to Syracuse, he had led both teams with 24 points and 11 rebounds.

Then, in a second-round loss to the University of Nevada at Las Vegas (UNLV) in the NCAA tournament, the Hoyas held the Runnin' Rebels to just 37.9 percent shooting from the field. UNLV was the defending national champion, and it was only the third time the team had

been held below 40 percent shooting in two seasons.

Alonzo finished the season with scoring (15.8 points per game) and rebounding (7.7) averages below those of his sophomore year. After the season, several college stars, such as Kenny Anderson of Georgia Tech and Billy Owens of Syracuse, announced they would be leaving school early to enter the NBA draft. Because Alonzo had had two frustrating seasons back to back, some people expected him to also leave school early and turn pro. But Alonzo announced that he would remain at Georgetown and graduate.

He said he wanted to be a center again and would have that chance next season, after Dikembe graduated. He felt he also had more to learn in college — about basketball and about life.

HEAD TO HEAD

Both Alonzo and Patrick Ewing are much better scorers in the pros than they were in college. Alonzo averaged 16.7 points per game during his career at Georgetown, and 21.2 points per game as a player in the NBA. Patrick averaged 15.3 points at Georgetown, and has averaged 23.7 points in nine seasons in the NBA.

BETTER THAN EVER

After the strain of his junior season, Alonzo was tired. Coach Thompson told him to relax over the summer of 1991. "I told him he needed to play basketball for fun," Coach Thompson said. "He needed to take some time off and enjoy himself."

Alonzo spent a lot of time in Washington. He worked in the office of a congressman on Capitol Hill. He also spent a lot of time at the Georgetown gym, working out with Patrick and Dikembe. Dikembe had been a first-round draft choice of the NBA's Denver Nuggets.

For two hours a day, five to six days a week, the three centers lifted weights and ran together. They helped each other develop new moves in practice and challenged each other in pickup games with other Hoya players.

Alonzo remembered how much fun playing ball could be. "Working out with Patrick and Dikembe all summer was great," he said. "Patrick's a gym rat. It's fascinating, really, that a man who makes so much money is such a gym rat. He's the perfect person to work out with."

When his senior season began, Alonzo was excited to be back on the court. He was the team captain, he was happy to be playing center, and a summer without playing organized basketball had left him, he said, "like a volcano ready to erupt."

Alonzo got off to a fast start, and never let up. After the first month and a half of the season, he was leading the nation in blocked shots (with an average of 5.6 per game), was fifth in rebounding (an average of 12.6), and was ninth in field-goal percentage (.670).

That year's Hoyas were young and inexperienced and Alonzo had to be their leader. His experience as a power forward had made him a very mobile, versatile center. Often, he was the Hoyas' whole show — blocking shots and grabbing defensive rebounds, hitting jump shots and hook shots, and grabbing offensive rebounds and slamming the ball into the basket.

Alonzo was much more focused. On off-days, Coach Thompson had to chase him out of the weight room. On the court, there was no trash talking and no bullying — Alonzo just outworked everyone else. "Look, I was young," Alonzo said of his old behavior on the court. "I wasn't smart. I'm looking at the game now mentally as much as physically. I was looking to overpower everybody before. Now, I'm trying to treat it like a chess game."

Alonzo didn't smile much on the court. Some people said he was scowling, but Alonzo said he was just

being serious. "When I hit the floor, it's me, my teammates, and our opponent," he would explain later. "I want
guys looking at me thinking they've got their hands full."

Averaging more than 23 points per game, Alonzo
led Georgetown to a 17–6 record (10–4 against the Big
East teams) by the end of February and the Number 18
ranking in the Associated Press college basketball poll. In
an upset of Syracuse at the Carrier Dome in Syracuse,
Alonzo had 27 points and 6 blocks. That made the Hoyas
the top team in the Big East conference.

Alonzo led the Big East in field goal percentage and
blocked shots, finished second in rebounding, and fourth
in scoring. He was named the Big East Player of the Year
and the Big East Tournament Most Valuable Player.

In the 1992 NCAA tournament, Alonzo carried the
hopes of the Hoyas as far as he could. In their first-round
victory over the University of South Florida, he scored 21
points, grabbed 11 rebounds, and blocked 6 shots.

In the second-round game, however, against Florida
State University, Alonzo was double-teamed in the first
half and scored just one point. In the second half, he
scored 13 points, but his teammates were shut down.
Georgetown lost, 78–68, and was eliminated from the tournament. Alonzo's college basketball career was over.

Alonzo finished his career as Georgetown's fourth-
leading scorer, third-leading rebounder, and second-leading shot-blocker. He became just the second Hoya player,

after Patrick, to score more than 2,000 points and grab more than 1,000 rebounds.

He was named a first team All-America. And although he didn't win any of the college player of the year awards, Alonzo had finally put together the kind of season he knew he was capable of.

He graduated from Georgetown that spring with a degree in sociology, which is the study of how groups of people behave. His parents, Fannie Threet, and Coach Thompson were at his graduation ceremony to watch him receive his college diploma.

NBA scouts expected Alonzo to be one of the first picks in the upcoming draft. The pro scouts, who had begun to doubt Alonzo's abilities after his junior season at Georgetown, were now praising him. Marty Blake, the NBA's director of scouting, said "He's going to be an outstanding pro player."

When the lottery was held in May, the Orlando Magic won the first pick and the Charlotte Hornets won the second choice. The Magic announced they would pick Shaquille O'Neal, the 7' 1" center from Louisiana State University. The Hornets said they would take Alonzo.

The Hornets wanted to build their team around Alonzo and forward Larry Johnson. The Hornets had chosen Larry with the number 1 pick in the draft the year before and he had become the NBA's rookie of the year. At the NBA draft, on June 24 in Portland, Oregon, the

Hornets made Alonzo their official first round selection.

Both Alonzo and the Hornets said they wanted to sign a contract right away and get ready for the season, but they couldn't agree on a salary. Alonzo's contract negotiations dragged on into the summer, through training camp, and up to the start of the season. Rather than sitting at home waiting for a contract, Alonzo was getting ready for the season by working out at Georgetown.

When the Hornets began their season on November 6, Alonzo was still in Georgetown. Both sides refused to budge. Then Coach Thompson talked to Hornet owner George Shinn, and a week later, Alonzo signed a contract with Charlotte that would pay him $25.2 million over six years, an average of $4.2 million per year.

Alonzo was set to travel with the team to Indianapolis on November 13 and suit up for that night's game against the Indiana Pacers. "The pressure is off me," said Mr. Shinn. "Now it's on the big guy."

HEAD TO HEAD

Patrick and Alonzo are ranked one and two in several categories in the Georgetown record book. Alonzo holds the record for most blocked shots in a season (169); Patrick is second (135). Patrick holds the record for most blocked shots in a college career (493); Alonzo is second (453).

THE ROOKIE
TAKES CHARGE

Charlotte Hornet fans were buzzing with excitement on the night of November 13 as Alonzo got ready to play his first game for the team. How would he do after missing training camp and the first four games of the season?

It didn't take long to find out. Playing in Indianapolis against the Pacers, Alonzo took the Hornets' first shot of the game, missed, and kept on firing. He scored Charlotte's first basket — and his first in the NBA — on a 15-foot jump shot. He either shot or committed a turnover the first 12 times he touched the ball. Early foul trouble kept him on the bench for much of the first half and almost all of the third quarter, but he finished with 12 points, 3 rebounds, and 1 blocked shot in 19 minutes of play. The Hornets lost a squeaker, 110–109, but Alonzo's teammates were glad he was finally playing with them.

"If it wasn't for him, we wouldn't even have been in the game," said Larry Johnson. "There's a lot of things he needs to work on, but he's going to be a great player. He

stepped right in and got right into it."

Alonzo said that he was a little anxious in his first game, but didn't feel any pressure. "All I have to do is stay focused and not worry about the expectations of the people outside the [Hornet] organization," he said.

After his first 11 games, Alonzo was averaging 16 points, 8.6 rebounds, and 3 blocks a game. He had posted a career-high 34 points against Golden State, and had helped the Hornets to a five-game winning streak. He had also made a lot of rookie mistakes, though, and Coach Allan Bristow felt he took too many long outside shots.

Alonzo made another rookie mistake in the Hornets' locker room after a loss to the Phoenix Suns on December 9. He asked Aileen Voisin, a female reporter from the Atlanta *Journal-Constitution*, to leave the room while he got dressed. The NBA has a rule that allows men and women reporters equal access to locker rooms. When Ms. Voisin refused to leave, Alonzo spoke rudely to her. Larry Johnson told Alonzo to stop it. Later, Alonzo apologized to the reporter.

One of his teammates explained that Alonzo was just being Alonzo. "He's an aggressive personality, no question, sometimes to a fault," said Mike Gminski, the Hornets' backup center. "On the court, he's going to make mistakes because of that. But what you see is what you get — he practices the same way he plays."

On December 10, 1992, the Hornets arrived in New

York for a game against the Knicks. It would be the first time, outside of the Georgetown gym, that Alonzo would go head-to-head with his idol, Patrick Ewing. Both players were excited. Alonzo and the Hornets more than held their own, upsetting the Knicks in overtime, 110–103.

Showing he wouldn't back down from anyone, Alonzo got into his first NBA fight, with Detroit Pistons' center Bill Laimbeer, just before Christmas. The season was barely two months old. Alonzo knew that fighting didn't prove anything, but he wanted to let the other NBA players know that he wasn't a rookie who could be pushed around.

In January, Alonzo fractured a bone in his thumb, but he refused to sit out any games. "It is slowing the healing process," he said. "But I'll sacrifice to win."

The fractured thumb didn't slow Alonzo down on the court. He had nine blocked shots in a victory against the world champion Chicago Bulls, and 34 points and 14 rebounds in a home win against Golden State. By the end of January, his scoring average was up to 18.7 points per game, his rebounding to 9.7, and his blocks to 3.92. The Hornets were having their best season ever, winning about half of their games.

Like Patrick Ewing, when he first came in the NBA, Alonzo was surprising everyone with his scoring. But it was his defense that Alonzo was most proud of. "You have to stop the other team from scoring," Alonzo said. "If you

stop people, you're going to get more shots for yourself. If you start the game with defense, offense will come to you."

It was another rookie center, Shaquille O'Neal of the Orlando Magic, who was voted by fans to start in the 1993 NBA All-Star Game in February. Shaquille was 7' tall, weighed more than 300 pounds, and was just 20 years old. He played like a man but sometimes acted like a big kid, and the fans and the media loved him. Alonzo didn't let Shaquille's popularity bother him. "To tell you the truth, my man," he told a reporter, "I really don't care how much attention Shaquille gets. I'm just concerned about winning."

Alonzo got even better as the season went on. By early April, he was averaging 20 points and 10.3 rebounds per game. He had already broken the Hornets career record for blocked shots.

People around the NBA compared Alonzo to Shaquille, and often gave Alonzo higher grades. "[Alonzo has] a much more all-around game than Shaq," said Knick forward Anthony Mason. "I'm sure Shaq is going to be a great player in this league, but as far as Shaq is concerned right now, he can't touch Alonzo. You don't have to worry about [Shaq] going out there and shooting the jumper or driving around you. [But] there's nothing Alonzo can't do."

By the time the regular season had ended, Alonzo

had boosted his per-game averages to 21.5 points, 10.3 rebounds, and 3.6 blocks. He had set a Hornet rookie record for most points scored (1,639), breaking Larry Johnson's mark, and a team record for blocked shots (271). More important to him, though, was that the Hornets had made the playoffs for the first time in their four-year history. Their 44–38 record was the best in club history. Shaquille beat out Alonzo to win the NBA Rookie of the Year award, but Alonzo was the *only* one of the top nine rookies in the draft whose team made the playoffs!

Charlotte's first playoff opponent was the Boston Celtics in a best-of-five-games series (the first team to win three games wins). Boston center Robert Parish, who was 17 years older than Alonzo, had averaged more than 20 points and 10 rebounds in his three regular-season meetings with the Hornet rookie. Two of those games were won by the Celtics.

But Alonzo was still getting better. In Game 2, the two teams battled each other through two overtime periods. Alonzo scored 18 points, grabbed 14 rebounds, and blocked 6 shots as Charlotte won, 99–98.

Game 3 was the first playoff game ever in Charlotte. Georgetown coach John Thompson came to the game. He waved to Alonzo before sitting down, and Alonzo responded by scoring 10 of his team's first 14 points. The Hornets won the game easily, 119–89.

The Hornets needed one more win to capture the

series. But as Game 4 wound down, Boston was ahead, 103–102. With just three seconds left to play, Hornet guard Del Curry inbounded the ball to Alonzo, who was coming around the top of the key. Alonzo caught the pass, faced the basket and launched a 20-foot jumper. He lost his balance and fell to the floor as the ball sailed through the air. But his aim was true. The ball swished into the basket just before the horn sounded to end the game! The Hornets had won their biggest game ever!

But the Hornets didn't have much time to celebrate. Their opponents in the second round of the playoffs would be Patrick Ewing and the New York Knicks. Alonzo and Patrick had met four times on the court during the season, with the Knicks winning three of those games. In those head-to-head battles, Patrick had averaged 35 points per game, and Alonzo almost 25. But, after all those summer practice games at Georgetown, the two centers knew each other's style of play better than that.

Alonzo reminded reporters that Patrick was the guy he'd looked up to since junior high school, then added, "But after the jump ball goes up, all that excitement and mentor stuff goes out the window. He understands that, too. He understands that both of us are out there, we're scrapping, trying to win. That's what it's all about. We'll talk about all that other stuff after the game."

This was a best of seven series; the first team to win four games would advance in the playoffs. Patrick's

Knicks won the first game, 111–95, at Madison Square
Garden. Hornet star forward Larry Johnson had to leave
the game early with an injury, which put the responsibility
squarely on Alonzo's back. He kept the game close until
the fourth quarter, scoring 27 points and impressing
everyone with his determination.

"For however long this Eastern Conference semifinal lasts," wrote reporter Harvey Araton in *The New York
Times*, "Patrick Ewing has to wrestle with his Georgetown
summer sparring partner [Alonzo] who goes after Ewing
like some little brother who's just figured out that he's big
enough to fight back."

In Game 2, the Hornets were ahead by 13 points
with less than seven minutes to play. But the Knicks came
back to win in overtime, 105–101. Alonzo led the Hornets
with 24 points, but Patrick had 34 points and an assist on
the winning shot by Knick rookie Hubert Davis.

The series moved to Charlotte for Game 3, and
another tough battle. This game went into double-overtime! But the Hornets hung in there. Alonzo and 5' 3"
guard Muggsy Bogues combined to score 12 of
Charlotte's 16 points in the two overtime periods, and the
Hornets won the game!

Alonzo scored 34 points and held Patrick under 30
for the first time in the series. Patrick had been in foul
trouble but he refused to use that as an excuse. "Alonzo
outplayed me tonight, fouls or no fouls," he said.

Still, Patrick and the Knicks had too much experience and talent for Alonzo and the Hornets. New York bounced back to win Game 4 in Charlotte, 94–92. Alonzo was held to 12 points and 8 rebounds. And when the series returned to New York for Game 5, the Knicks finished off the Hornets, 105–101. Alonzo gave his all, scoring 22 points and grabbing 12 rebounds.

After the game, Alonzo and Patrick hugged each other at center court. Alonzo wished Patrick and the Knicks well the rest of the way in the playoffs. If Alonzo couldn't win the championship this year, he wanted it to go to Patrick.

In just his rookie year, Alonzo had already shown he belonged in the battle with the NBA's best.

HEAD TO HEAD

Georgetown University is the only college to have three former players as starting centers in the NBA: Alonzo with the Charlotte Hornets, Patrick Ewing with the New York Knicks, and Dikembe Mutombo with the Denver Nuggets.

A STAR
IN HIS OWN
LIGHT

Alonzo Mourning was very busy over the summer of 1993. He bought homes for his mom, his dad, and his foster mother, Fannie Threet. He also spent a lot of time working with kids. Alonzo helps out with a Charlotte organization that tries to prevent child abuse. He runs basketball clinics for a kids' program in the Virgin Islands called "Stop The Violence," and he participates in Special Olympics activities.

He was also back in the Georgetown gym with Patrick Ewing and Dikembe Mutombo—working out hard. "Watch them go against each other in pickup games," Georgetown Coach John Thompson told a reporter, "and you'll swear they're going to fight."

In August, Alonzo went to Los Angeles to play in a charity basketball game (for the United Negro College Fund) that former Laker star Magic Johnson puts on each year. The game always draws a big crowd. This one was

special because it gave people a chance to watch Alonzo and Shaquille O'Neal go at each other.

Magic's all-star game is played for fun. The stars show the fans what they can do, and nobody really plays defense. When the game was all over, Shaquille had outscored Alonzo, 45 points to 29 points, but Alonzo had given Shaquille something to remember him by.

On one play, Shaq drove to the basket and wound up for a thunderous dunk. Fans practically held their breath, as if Shaq was going to bring the building crashing down.

But the next thing anyone knew, there was Alonzo, leaping high to block the shot back into Shaquille and send the 7-foot, 300-pound big man sprawling onto the court! Ten minutes later, Shaq went in for another slam dunk, and Alonzo put him on his tail again!

Later, Alonzo insisted there was nothing special for him about playing against the Orlando center. "Any player who tries to keep me from doing what I want motivates me, not just Shaq," he said. Still, it seemed like Alonzo was trying to send a message to Shaquille and the rest of the NBA: Charity game or playoff game, nobody gets an easy basket against Alonzo Mourning.

Alonzo's aggressive style had already earned him a reputation around the NBA. "Nobody in the league likes to play against Zo," said Hornet Muggsy Bogues, referring to Alonzo by his nickname. "He works so hard at his

game, and his aggressiveness gets under people's skin."

Players and coaches also respected him for his talent. "I think [Alonzo] can be a 30-point scorer," said Knick coach Pat Riley. "He scores in every facet of the game. . . . He runs well and he scores off movement, off post-ups, and off second shots. He can score from the line and keep you honest with his jumper."

Coach Riley said Alonzo reminded him of — who else? — Patrick Ewing. And that summer, just as Patrick had been a member of the Dream Team that won an Olympic gold medal in Barcelona in 1992, Alonzo and teammate Larry Johnson were named to Dream Team II, the all-star team that would represent the U. S. at the 1994 world championships.

When the 1993–94 season began, the Hornets had huge expectations. "I truly believe we are a team of destiny," said team owner George Shinn. "With players like Alonzo and Larry, I believe this team will win a championship."

So it was disappointing to the Hornets and their fans when the team sleep-walked to a 1–3 start. But when the Orlando Magic came to town the Hornets woke up. Thanks to Alonzo's defense and the defensive help of his teammates, Charlotte held Shaq to just 19 points (he went into the game averaging 38.3) and won the game, 120–87.

The win gave the Hornets some sting. The next night they beat the Celtics at Boston Garden. Alonzo

scored 23 points and grabbed 17 rebounds. He even enjoyed the fans' attempt behind the basket to distract him when he was shooting free throws.

"To be truthful, I love it," he said. "The fans won't harass somebody they don't respect. If they respect and appreciate your game, they're going to try to get to you. They do the same thing to Charles Barkley."

The Hornets went on to win 8 of 11 games. They even moved into first place in the NBA's Central Division. Alonzo was averaging 21.7 points and 10.1 rebounds per game. At one point, he was tenth in scoring in the league.

But the Hornets soon discovered that nobody was going to just hand them a ticket to the NBA Finals just because they were young and worked hard.

First, after a slow start, some of the older and more experienced teams in the Central Division, where Charlotte played, began to play up to their abilities. The Atlanta Hawks caught fire and won 15 straight games. The Chicago Bulls, who had lost Michael Jordan to retirement, began to show people they were still a good team. The Hornets dropped down into third place.

Then in December both Alonzo and Larry Johnson went down with injuries. Alonzo badly sprained an ankle, and Larry was having pains in his back. Together, Alonzo and Larry had been averaging over 40 points a game, more than one third of the Hornets' offense.

Alonzo came back and played well, scoring 30

points in back-to-back games, but then he suffered another leg injury, this time a torn calf muscle. He was named to play in the 1994 All-Star Game, right around his 24th birthday. He and Patrick Ewing would have been All-Star teammates! But because of his injury, Alonzo was unable to play.

The injury kept Alonzo out of action for 15 games. Without him and Larry playing, the Hornets lost 14 of those games. When Alonzo returned to the starting lineup on March 8, the Hornets had a record of 24–33 and had fallen to fifth place in the Central Division. In his first game back, Alonzo scored 24 points to help the Hornets defeat the Phoenix Suns and end an eight-game losing streak.

Larry returned to action in the next game, and for the first time since late December, the Hornets had their two stars in the lineup at the same time. But they had a long, uphill climb to make in order to reach the playoffs.

Despite an impressive record of 10-4 in April and 18–8 overall with Alonzo back in the lineup, the Hornets couldn't make into the NBA postseason The team finished the season with a 41–41 record, a game behind the Miami Heat for the last playoff spot in the Eastern Conference.

It was disappointing for the team to miss the playoffs. But there was reason to be hopeful about the future Alonzo led the team in scoring (21.5), rebounding (10.2), and blocks (3.13). His blocks ranked him fourth in the

NBA. Without Alonzo in the lineup, the team was 6–16; with him, their record was 35–23. In only his second professional season, Alonzo was clearly becoming a dominant player in the NBA.

* * *

Alonzo has quickly become an important player in the NBA, not only for his scoring and defense, but for the intensity and positive attitude he brings to his team.

From the ups and downs in his life, Alonzo has learned to be himself, and not to focus on what others want him to be. "If you go through life worried about what people think about you all the time, [you'll find] you can't please everybody," he says.

Instead, Alonzo is concentrating on what he wants, which is to be a winner. And he is willing to work as hard as he has to in order to become one. "I read where someone said, 'The harder you work, the luckier you get,'" he says. "I want to be the luckiest person in basketball."

When he finishes his career, Alonzo would like to start an organization that helps children, just as Ms. Threet helped him when he was a kid. But first, there is the matter of winning a championship. He's been waiting since high school for that one. And if he has to, he'll take the ball and dunk right over his good friend Patrick Ewing to get it.

ALONZO MOURNING'S CAREER STATS

COLLEGE STATS
Georgetown University

SEASONS	Games	POINTS		REBOUNDS		BLKS	
		Total	Avg	Total	Avg.	Total	Avg.
1988–89	34	447	13.2	248	7.3	169	4.9
1989–90	31	510	16.5	265	8.5	69	2.2
1990–91	23	363	15.8	176	7.7	55	2.3
1991–92	37	681	21.7	343	10.7	160	5.0
Totals	143	2,001	16.7	1,032	8.5	453	3.6

PRO STATS
Charlotte Hornets

SEASONS	Games	POINTS		REBOUNDS		BLKS	
		Total	Avg.	Total	Avg.	Total	Avg.
1992–93	78	1,639	21.0	805	10.3	271	3.4
1993–94	60	1,287	21.5	610	8.8	188	3.1
Totals	138	2,926	21.2	1,415	9.5	459	3.2